MANIFESTO FOR A POST-CRITICAL PEDAGOGY

BEFORE YOU START TO READ THIS BOOK, take this moment to think about making a donation to punctum books, an independent non-profit press,

@ https://punctumbooks.com/support/

If you're reading the e-book, you can click on the image below to go directly to our donations site. Any amount, no matter the size, is appreciated and will help us to keep our ship of fools afloat. Contributions from dedicated readers will also help us to keep our commons open and to cultivate new work that can't find a welcoming port elsewhere. Our adventure is not possible without your support.

Vive la open-access.

Fig. 1. Hieronymus Bosch, *Ship of Fools* (1490–1500)

First published in 2017 by punctum books, Earth, Milky Way.
https://punctumbooks.com

ISBN-13: 978-1-947447-38-7 (print)
ISBN-13: 978-1-947447-39-4 (ePDF)

LCCN: 2017961281
Library of Congress Cataloging Data is available from the Library of Congress

Book design: Vincent W.J. van Gerven Oei

HIC SVNT MONSTRA

Manifesto for a Post-Critical Pedagogy

Naomi Hodgson
Joris Vlieghe
Piotr Zamojski

Contents

Introduction · 11
Naomi Hodgson, Joris Vlieghe, and Piotr Zamojski

MANIFESTO FOR A POST-CRITICAL PEDAGOGY

Manifesto for a Post-Critical Pedagogy · 15
Naomi Hodgson, Joris Vlieghe, and Piotr Zamojski

RESPONSES

A Response to the
"Manifesto for A Post-Critical Pedagogy" · · · · · · · · · · · · · · · · 23
Tyson E. Lewis

A Sociologist's Conversation with the
"Manifesto for a Post-Critical Pedagogy" · · · · · · · · · · · · · · · · · 35
Olga Ververi

Towards a Pedagogical Hermeneutics: A Response to the
"Manifesto for a Post-Critical Pedagogy" · · · · · · · · · · · · · · · · · 43
Norm Friesen

Differences That Might Matter?
A Manifesto Diffractively Read · 49
Geert Thyssen

The Post-Critical Mind as a Gateway to
Embodied Hope and Love for the World · · · · · · · · · · · · · · · · · ·57
Oren Ergas

Love for the World in Education ·63
Stefan Ramaekers

POST-CRITIQUE

Post-Critique: A Conversation between
Naomi Hodgson, Joris Vlieghe, and Piotr Zamojski· · · · · · · · ·71

Contributors ·103

Introduction

Naomi Hodgson, Joris Vlieghe, and Piotr Zamojski

The *Manifesto for a Post-Critical Pedagogy* was written in September 2016 and first presented at Liverpool Hope University on October 17, 2016. At that launch event, we heard a keynote response from Tyson Lewis and further invited responses from Geert Thyssen and Olga Ververi. From the outset, having made the manifesto available online in open access, we were encouraged by the enthusiastic response and the genuine interest shown by colleagues internationally. We therefore chose to invite further responses, to broaden the conversation, but did so specifically from early- to mid-career scholars. Hence, we also include here responses from Oren Ergas, Norm Friesen, and Stefan Ramaekers.

When seeking a way to publish the manifesto and the responses to it, we looked purposefully beyond the usual avenues taken in our field, for a publisher in keeping with the ethos of the manifesto itself. We thank punctum books and Eileen Joy and Vincent W.J. van Gerven Oei in particular for the confidence and enthusiasm they have shown in this project.

The strong commitment to open access publishing by punctum books is part of a shifting environment for academic publishing in which the demands of visibility and metrics compete with, and compromise, the public dimension of *public*ation in academia. We are grateful to Liverpool Hope University for the Higher Education Impact Funding we received to support the cost not only of publication but also of maintaining the book in open access in perpetuity.

We would also like to thank the Centre for Higher Education and Policy Analysis (CEPA) at Liverpool Hope University and the Philosophy of Education Society of Great Britain (PESGB) for their support in hosting and funding the launch seminar.

We provide no commentary here on the manifesto itself, or the responses that follow it in this book, other than to say that, as a manifesto it is intended to be short and to contain no references. The responses are more academic in style but still adopt a more conversational tone than a regular text, and they vary in length. The conversation form is taken up more fully in the final chapter in which we seek to address some of the questions they raise in ways that, we hope, provide further provocation and keep the conversation open.

MANIFESTO FOR A POST-CRITICAL PEDAGOGY

Manifesto for a Post-Critical Pedagogy

Naomi Hodgson, Joris Vlieghe, and Piotr Zamojski

Formulating principles, in philosophy of education at least, seems to hark back to a form of normative, conceptual analysis associated with Anglophone, analytic styles of philosophy. But poststructuralist and postmodernist philosophy — at least as they have been taken up in educational theory and in popular thought more generally — often brings with it a relativism, which while potentially inclusive, and certainly constitutive today of the possibility of individual choice, renders the defence of principles difficult. By stating principles in the form of a manifesto, we risk accusations of universalising, exclusive normativity. But, it is perhaps time to question the assumption that these are inherently and always negative. Below we set out principles founded in the belief in the possibility of transformation, as found in critical theory and pedagogy, but with an affirmative attitude: a post-critical orientation to education that gains purchase on our current conditions and that is founded in a hope for what is still to come.

The **first principle** to state here is simply that **there are principles to defend**. But this does not in itself commit us to anything further, i.e., that we ought to do x. This is not normativity in the sense of defining an ideal current or future state against which current practice should be judged. Thus, this principle might be characterised as the defence of a shift from **procedural normativity to principled normativity**.

In educational theory, poststructuralist and postmodernist thought has often been taken up in terms of the politics of identity, and so a concern with otherness, alterity, and voice. Respect for the other and for difference requires that educators accept that we can never fully know the other. Any attempt to do so constitutes "violence" against the other, so to speak. Thus, the possibility of acting and speaking is foreclosed; a political as well as an educational problem, perhaps summarised in the often heard (albeit mumbled) phrase "I know you're not allowed to say this anymore, but...," and the bemoaning of so-called political correctness. The acceptance that we can never fully understand the other — individual or culture — ought not to entail that we cannot speak. This rendering of "respect" overlooks that understanding and respect are perpetual challenges and hopes. Here, we start from the assumption that we can speak and act — together — and thus shift from the hermeneutical pedagogy that critical pedagogy entails, to defend a — **second principle — pedagogical hermeneutics**. It is precisely the challenges of living together in a common world that constitute the hope that make education continue to seem a worthwhile activity. Hermeneutics isn't a (unsolvable) problem, but rather something educators need to create. We shouldn't speak and act on the basis of a priori assumptions about the (im)possibility of real mutual understanding and respect, but rather show that, in spite of the many differences that divide us, there is a space of commonality that only comes about a posteriori (cf. Arendt, Badiou, Cavell).

This existing space of commonality is often overlooked in much educational research, policy, and practice in favour of a focus on social (in)justice and exclusion, based on an assumption of inequality. The ethos of critical pedagogy endures today in the commitment to achieving equality, not through emancipation, but rather through empowerment of individuals and communities. However, it is rendered hopeless — not to mention, cynical — by the apparent inescapability of neoliberal rationality. But, there is no *necessity* in the given order of things, and thus, insurmountable as the current order seems, there is hope. The **third principle**, then, based on the assumption of equality (cf. Rancière) and of the possibility of transformation — at the individual and collective levels — entails a shift **from critical pedagogy to post-critical pedagogy**.

This is by no means an anti-critical position. It is thanks to the enormous and extremely powerful critical apparatus developed throughout the 20th century that we are aware of the main features of the status quo we are immersed in. But, unlike the inherent critique of societal institutions focused on their dysfunctionality, or the utopian critique, driven from a transcendent position and leading towards eternal deferral of the desired change, we believe that it is time to focus our efforts on making attempts to reclaim the suppressed parts of our experience; we see the task of a post-critical pedagogy as not to debunk but to protect and to care (cf. Latour, Haraway). This care and protection take the form of asking again what education, upbringing, school, studying, thinking, and practicing are. This reclaiming entails no longer a critical relation — revealing what is really going on — nor an instrumental relation — showing what educators ought to do — but creating a space of thought that enables practice to happen anew. This means (re)establishing our relation to our words, opening them to question, and giving philosophical attention to these devalued aspects of our forms of life, and thus — in line with a principled normativity — to defend these events as autotelic, not functionalised, but simply worth caring for.

Education is, in a very practical sense, predicated on hope. In "traditional" critical pedagogy, however, this hope of emancipation rests on the very regime of inequality it seeks to overcome, in three particular ways:

1. It enacts a kind of hermeneutical pedagogy: the educator assumes the other to lack the means to understand that they are chained by their way of seeing the world. The educator positions herself as external to such a condition, but must criticize the present and set the unenlightened free (cf. Plato's cave).

2. In reality this comes down to reaffirming one's own superior position, and thus to reinstalling a regime of inequality. There is no real break with the status quo.

3. Moreover, the external point of view from which the critical pedagogue speaks is through and through chained to the status quo, but in a merely negative way: the critic is driven by the passion of hate. In doing so, she or he surreptitiously sticks to what is and what shall always be. Judgmental and dialectical approaches testify to this negative attitude.

Thus, the pedagogue assumes the role of one who is required to lift the veil; what they lift the veil from, however, is a status quo on which they stand in external judgment. To formulate more positively the role of the pedagogue as initiating the new generation into a common world, we offer the idea of a post-critical pedagogy, which requires a love for the world. This is not an acceptance of how things are, but an affirmation of the value of what we do in the present and thus of things that we value as worth passing on. But not as they are: educational hope is about the possibility of a renewal of our common world. When we truly love the world, our world, we must be willing to pass it on to the new generation, on the assumption that they — the newcomers — can take it on, on their terms. Thus, the **fourth principle** entails a shift **from cruel optimism** (cf. Berlant) **to hope in the present**. Cynicism and pessimism are not, in a sense, a recognition of how things are, but an avoidance of them (cf. Cavell, Emerson).

In current formulations, taking care of the world is framed in terms of education *for* citizenship, education *for* social justice, education *for* sustainability, etc. in view of a particular notion of global citizenship and an entrepreneurial form of intercultural dialogue. Although perhaps underpinned by a progressive, critical pedagogy, the concern in such formulations of responsibility for the world is with ends external to education. Traditional or conservative as it might sound, we wish to defend education for education's sake: education as the study of, or initiation into, a subject matter for its intrinsic, educational, rather than instrumental, value, so that this can be taken up anew by the new generation. Currently, the (future) world is already appropriated by "education *for...*" and becomes instrumental to (our) other ends. Thus, **the fifth principle** takes us **from education for citizenship to love for the world**. It is time to acknowledge and to affirm that there is good in the world that is worth preserving. It is time for debunking the world to be succeeded by some hopeful recognition of the world. It is time to put what is good in the world — that which is under threat and which we wish to preserve — at the centre of our attention and to make a conceptual space in which we can take up our responsibility for them in the face of, and in spite of, oppression and silent melancholy.

RESPONSES

1

A Response to the "Manifesto for A Post-Critical Pedagogy"

Tyson E. Lewis

First, I would like to thank Hodgson, Vlieghe, and Zamojski for inviting me to this event and for allowing me to engage with their ideas. But I must admit that I almost felt like this was a set-up or an ironic gesture. How can I give a critical response to a post-critical manifesto without immediately falling prey to the very problems of critique that the authors identify? If I provide a critical analysis, then would my response even be relevant? Could I not immediately be dismissed as symptomatic of a failure in educational philosophy to produce affirmative principles? And if the response cannot be critical without falling into a trap, need it simply be an affirmation, meaning a repetition of what has already been said? If this were the case, then I need not continue as my response would be redundant. I can merely pack my bags and head home. Both critique and simple affirmation seem unsatisfactory at this point, and would fail to take up the call for a creative hermeneutic that has to be produced. As such, my only real choice in writing this response is to utilize the principles of post-critique in order to care for post-critique. Such care need not simply be an affirmation. Rather, it can point to that which the authors have failed to care about in their own call to care, and thus can further develop an underdeveloped aspect of their post-critical turn. The resulting paper is my attempt to respond to post-critique by caring for that which is present in the author's statement and yet remains marginal and peripheral: the question of aesthetic form.

Hodgson, Vlieghe, and Zamojski have provided us with an evocative manifesto for a post-critical pedagogy. They highlight the deficiencies with three dominant trends in educational philosophy: Anglophone/analytic; poststructuralist; and critical schools of thought. Analytic forms of educational philosophy fall prey to charges of exclusivity and/or ideal theory, which seems to foreclose on the possibility of the new from appearing precisely because principles have already been posited that define what the good is and how we ought to pursue it. At the other extreme of the spectrum, poststructuralism has left us with a world of only relative opinions and, thus, has eclipsed the common world of which we are a part. No longer can we posit any principles whatsoever, for all principles are the result of forms of power over and against someone or something. The result of this position is the splintering of the common into ever smaller and more selective sub-cultures and counter-publics, which might have had some progressive political and educational purposes at one time, but today, it seems that such fragmentation is part and parcel of the logic of global finance capitalism, which continually attempts to create niche markets for commodity exchange. Opposed to this logic of the market, we find critical pedagogy, which, as the authors point out, takes a transcendent position outside of the system of capitalism in order to denounce that which is. Here, we find the great refusal at work, a refusal that is predicated on dialectical negation in the name of a utopia to come. Such a position proclaims relative autonomy from circuits of capitalist production and consumption, yet, in this very same gesture, reproduces a kind of stultifying logic of inequality between the critical pedagogue, who has the correct political orientation and critical knowledge of how things really are, and the student, who is mystified by a naïve consciousness.

Hodgson, Vlieghe, and Zamojski offer up not merely an alternative, but an affirmative one at that. They shift the parameters of the debate from either a relativistic embrace of everything that is, or a critical denunciation of everything that is, to a position of caring for and protecting the world — not in the sense of merely accepting the status quo, but rather in the sense of valuing the present as containing the possibility of renewal of the commons as an inherent good in itself. This is a commons that is (a) denied by poststructuralists and (b) deferred into the future by both the analytic and critical schools. What the authors want to highlight is the common as it exists in the present.

There is much that I agree with in this manifesto, and many aspects of it dovetail nicely with my own interest in study.[1] In particular, I find it praiseworthy that the authors have provided an outline of a new approach to thinking through philosophy of education that is bold and has the potential to reorient the field toward new possibilities. What I would like to do here is spend the next couple of minutes thinking about the form of address the authors have chosen — the manifesto — and consider the educational and political implications of this choice. My assumption is that we cannot neglect to consider forms of writing as having educational importance. My question to the authors is thus: Does the content match the form? Is the manifesto adequate for articulating a post-analytic, post-post-structural, and post-critical educational philosophy?

When we think of educational modes of address that attempt to articulate principles for change, three come to mind. This is not an exhaustive list by any means. Rather, it is an attempt to provide a topology of forms of writing so that we can begin to understand how different forms have different pedagogical implications. First, there is the educational creed. Perhaps the most famous creed was proposed by John Dewey. Published in 1897 in *School Journal*, Dewey's creed is important not so much in relation to its contents — which he more eloquently spells out in any number of other places — as its mode of address. The creed is a *personal testimony* to held beliefs. In this sense, the "my" in Dewey's title, "My Pedagogic Creed," is redundant for

---

1   Tyson Lewis, *On Study: Giorgio Agamben and Educational Potentiality* (New York: Routledge, 2013).

all creeds are of a personal, and thus individual, nature. Groups and institutions do not usually have creeds. Each statement in Dewey's creed begins with "I believe x." Dewey thus emphasizes that each statement is not a statement of fact, or of a collective standpoint, so much as his opinion. Granted, this opinion is a learned one, but the point remains: the creed belongs to someone, it is someone's perspective.

The impact of Dewey's creed on current teacher education should not be underestimated. There are any number of articles describing its impact on the public's perception of the role of schools in promoting social change, as well as articles describing the relationship between the creed and Dewey's later, more philosophically robust, books on education, democracy, and the school. Yet, in my review of Dewey's creed, no one seems to have paused to point out the form of the creed itself, and to speculate why Dewey chose this form. As a formal statement of personal belief, a creed is not a philosophy, nor is it a set of laws, nor is it a set of scientific principles. Rather, it is a passionate conviction that one holds. It conveys faith in something or someone. As such, the creed can be traced back to religious confession. For this reason, it is not at all surprising that Dewey would end his creed (which testifies to the powers of science and reason) with a religious turn of phrase: "I believe that in this way the teacher always is the prophet of the true God and the usherer in of the true kingdom of God."

As strange as it might sound, we live in an era in which the creed has increasing popularity, especially in teacher education. For instance, at my former university, it was required that all undergraduate, pre-service teachers write their own educational creed. This was not meant to be a philosophical statement, but rather a testimony to one's individual voice as an emerging teacher. But if the creed has religious roots, why have we seen its return in a "secular" age? The popularity of writing creeds in today's colleges of education (at least in the US) might very well have to do with the strangely postmodern logic of the creed. While there have been any number of scholars attempting to define or redefine Dewey's relation to the postmodern, what I find fascinating here is how the creed, which is a particularly Christian technology, can come to be reconfigured as a kind of postmodern pedagogic form that celebrates voices regardless of critical engagement with the content of the creeds. If the creed is nothing more than a personal set of beliefs, then how can one argue against it? Your creed is just as good as my creed. We seem to find ourselves in a state of relativism where creeds flourish, where personal belief triumphs. Everyone in teacher education must confess their creed, and we should all celebrate the creeds as statements of individuality. "I believe" overcomes "I argue" or "I have discovered."

And as creeds multiply, the commonwealth of the world withdraws, reducing educational thought to atomized, isolated confessions of faith. Another way of framing this would be to say that a creed cannot articulate shared principles to be de- fended, as Hodgson, Vlieghe, and Zamojski call for. When faced with opposition, the author of a creed can only say, "Well that is your opinion. You have your creed, and I have mine." As such, the world disappears behind a multiplicity of creeds; dialogue is replaced by monologue. For these reasons, there is some- thing refreshing about Hodgson, Vlieghe, and Zamojski's turn away from the creed to the manifesto. Such a move reorients educators away from personal, idiosyncratic, and introspective creeds toward the world of shared principles, dialogue, and the commons. The struggle with one's self to articulate a creed is replaced with a collective struggle over the world and which principles best care for it.

Another major form of address found in education is the charter. These are familiar documents for those in the US, who have witnessed the rise of the charter school movement. The charter is composed of fundamental principles that guide the running of schools. Thus, unlike the creed, the charter is col- lectively oriented. It also has a normative weight not attributed to creeds. Yet there is a key difference between the charter and Hodgson, Vlieghe, and Zamojski's manifesto that should be pointed out. First, as I have already hinted at, the charter con- cerns what Hodgson, Vlieghe, and Zamojski refer to as "procedural normativity." Stated differently, the charter is always about what the school *ought to do* or what parents and communities *ought to expect*. Charters convey normative ideals that communities can then reference in order to determine whether or not a certain school is living up to its own promises.

Second, charters are written by a legislative or sovereign power, by which an institution is created and its rights, duties, and privileges defined. As such, it is a binding, formal document that is guaranteed by a sovereign or legislative body. It is a contract. The status of the charter is secured by the law, and the security it offers is legally binding. What I find most important about Hodgson, Vlieghe, and Zamojski's manifesto is precisely its rejection of any certainty grounded in legislative or sovereign powers. Instead of legal powers, we have recourse to our common capacities for hermeneutic interpretations. This means that there are no guarantees; there is no recourse to higher powers over and above our own capacities for judgment and interpretation.

Third, Hodgson, Vlieghe, and Zamojski's manifesto is not institutionally bound. Indeed, the gesture toward the common and toward the world speaks to a philosophy of education that cannot be institutionalized without, in some way, privatizing that which is collective in nature. Their orientation is to the commonalities of the world that defy any institutional attempt to control or police. While it might very well be possible to form charters out of this commonwealth, this need not be the case, as the commons might challenge the forms of legal and sovereign powers that bring the charter into existence.

But if the document that Hodgson, Vlieghe, and Zamojski have written is neither a creed nor a charter, is it really a manifesto? If we think to manifestos in the past, they are certainly collective in nature, often describing the commitments of political or artistic or educational movements. They are also principled. Unlike creeds, they are articulations of positions to be argued over and debated. And unlike the charter, they are often illegal, or extra-legal, challenging a sovereign power that is held over and above them. I am thinking here of *The Manifesto of the Communist Party* written by Marx and Engels. That manifesto is exemplary in several respects. It is a collective endeavor to articulate not simply a personal set of beliefs but rather the standpoint of a class. It is polemic and, finally, it is illegal, transgressing any state or national laws. In these senses, the document produced by Hodgson, Vlieghe, and Zamojski does indeed appear to be a manifesto.

Yet at the same time, the manifesto is prophetic, future-oriented, and thus concerned with transformation toward some kind of alternative future state. Think here of Marx and Engels' manifesto. Its goal is to forecast certain trends in the ongoing class war in order to help shape and guide the revolution toward a post-capitalist state. The manifesto diagnoses, predicts, and ultimately orients us toward a dialectical negation of the present in the name of a communist future to come. The internal logic of the manifesto resembles the internal logic of critical pedagogy, hence the reason why the manifesto is the preferred platform for critical pedagogues such as Henry Giroux and Peter McLaren. To read critical pedagogy is to read manifestos, including "A Revolutionary Critical Pedagogy Manifesto for the Twenty-First Century" by Peter McLaren,[2] or "When Schools Become Deadzones of the Imagination: A Critical Pedagogy Manifesto" by Henry Giroux.[3] Such texts are full of proclamations describing what teachers ought to do in order to undermine the system and help actualize the promise of equality, democracy, and communism in a better tomorrow. As authors, McLaren and Giroux take on the role of prophets who forecast certain economic and social trends in order to enrage and inspire protest, all in the name of critical principles that the critical pedagogue must safeguard. They are prophets of doom and salvation, both of which

2   Matthew Smith, Jean Ryoo, and Peter McLaren, "A Revolutionary Critical Pedagogy Manifesto for the Twenty-First Century," *Education and Society* 27, no. 3 (2009): 59–76.

3   Henry A. Giroux, "When Schools Become Dead Zones of the Imagination: A Critical Pedagogy Manifesto," *Policy Futures in Education* 12, no. 4 (2014): 491–99. First published August 13, 2013 at truth-out.org, http://www.truth-out.org/news/item/18133-when-schools-become-dead-zones-of-the-imagination-a-critical-pedagogy-manifesto.

are always on the horizon, always approaching and receding in equal measure. Here, hope and doom are synthesized into an eschatological theory that is always fixated on crisis after crisis.

In this sense, the manifesto must make manifest that which is not present, that which is deferred. It does so through the authority of the prophet or seer who can forecast dystopian and utopian possibilities from the current situation. Interestingly, we could argue that the prophet takes the creed and makes private beliefs into a kind of charter; this time, a charter guaranteed by history, or God, or some other transcendent power that only speaks through the prophet as a chosen emissary.

Yet, on my reading, the document produced by Hodgson, Vlieghe, and Zamojski rejects not only Giroux and McLaren as representatives of critical pedagogy, but also, more importantly, undermines the authority of the prophet as well as the function of the manifesto, which is always oriented away from the present toward the future. Of course, the collective nature of the manifesto remains operative, but this is a collectivity that is present, now, and only needs to be verified rather than conjured up. As the authors write, the role of a post-critical pedagogy is "not to debunk but to protect and to care" for what is good in the present. The result is not hope in some kind of future in which freedom, equality, or democracy can be realized, so much as hope in the present for the freedom, equality, and democracy that exist but only need verification. Here, the authors seem to draw inspiration from Jacques Rancière's interpretation of the master-slave dialectic.[4] At the very heart of a relationship that defines inequality (slavery), Rancière finds a disavowed reliance upon the equality of intelligences; for how can the slave carry out the master's orders if he or she is not already capable of thinking and speaking? Likewise, the logic of the prophet is rejected as a stultifying educational position, a position that simultaneously

---

4   Jacques Rancière, *The Philosopher and His Poor,* ed. Andrew Parker, trans. John Drury, Corinne Oster, and Andrew Parker (Durham: Duke University Press, 2004).

(a) is predicated on an equality it disavows, while (b) continually reproducing an inequality that it needs.

In sum, if the manifesto is predicated on the authority of the prophet to predict a future that is guaranteed by God, or by the laws of history, then whatever Hodgson, Vlieghe, and Zamojski have produced cannot be called a manifesto. Their document does not make manifest in the form of a prediction, so much as it declares what is present in order to care for it. And this declaration is collective yet poor — poor in the sense that it does not have the recognition by the law or the sovereign or the prophet to support it and verify it. If this is a manifesto, then it is an inoperative one, or a manifesto at a standstill. Such a document does not tell us what to do, how to do it, or what will happen, so much as it opens the present to that which remains in potential and thus undestined for any particular use.

I would thus conclude with the suggestion that what Hodgson, Vlieghe, and Zamojski have produced is properly named a declaration. They are declaring that what is contains within itself a new potentiality that is not reducible to a personal belief, a legally recognized institutional form, or a prophetic vision of what is to come. Such a declaration does not tell us what to do, how to do it, or what will happen, so much as it maintains the open potentiality of the present for new use. This is what is most precious and fragile in the present. And for these reasons, potentiality is that which needs the most love.

If the authors simply embrace the form of the manifesto as their own and use it to articulate a post-critical pedagogy, then there is a danger that the formal elements defining the manifesto might return to undermine the content of their argument. I can see several ways in which the form of the manifesto returns to contaminate the content of this post-critical declaration. For instance, if the authors want a non-instrumental approach to education that does not submit education as a means to an external end, perhaps instrumentality returns in the form of responsibility, for it is unclear to me that responsibility is an inherently educational concept. Indeed, one could make the claim that it is, first and foremost, an ethical and political concern, which education helps us strive to achieve. And because of this, a telos is reintroduced back into the framework. The work of post-critical philosophy is therefore not to care for what is present so much as to make manifest that which ought to be. And finally, while the authors are careful to distinguish between cruel optimism and hope in the present, I would still suggest that hope is always oriented toward something to come and thus away from what is present. The formal features of the manifesto — instrumentality, teleology, and hope — thus seep back into the content of the document in the shape.

At the same time, there is a danger that if the authors invent an entirely new form of writing, then they will fail to care for and love the present. Instead of the present, they would be opting for a kind of avant-garde position where, again, the absent future is privileged and made manifest through new aesthetic forms. Such a position thus lies in contradiction with the content of their argument, which wants to remain immanent to the present without introducing the transcendent.

Yet there is a third path here — a path that is neither the reproduction of the manifesto nor the production of something new. This is the path of the declaration. The declaration is not simply a manifesto nor its negation. There is nothing old or new about the declaration. The declaration is an *occupation* of the manifesto in order to deactivate its formal features — instrumentality, teleology, and hope — and thus redeem its declarative use. Unlike the creed, the declaration is collective. It belongs to no one in particular. Unlike the charter, it is not bound to the law or the state for its guarantee. It rejects bureaucratization. And unlike the manifesto, it is grounded in the present and reflects this present back to itself in order to expose that which remains in potential. Also, it has its own affective qualities. If the creed concerns religious reverence, the charter concerns respect for the law, and the manifesto concerns rage and hope for a future, then the declaration concerns joy for what is in the present. Thus, one does not say, "I hope that my teaching will transform the world." This is a kind of future-oriented affect that leads to manifesto writing. Rather one says, "I find joy in the possibilities of teaching right now." This is a declaration of the potentiality that exists all around us.

On my reading, the declaration is a formal occupation of a space and a time of the manifesto by an alternative space and time that is most interesting, and in turn most educationally relevant. Yet when Hodgson, Vlieghe, and Zamojski fail to take into account the formal structure of their document, the form of the declaration remains underdeveloped and thus the spontaneous ideology of the manifesto seeps back in to contaminate the post-critical with the critical, the instrumental, the teleological, and the hopeful. In this sense, the form must be made into its own kind of content so that we can begin to understand how post-critique must take care of and preserve not only concepts but also modes of presentation.

As such, I would like to see the authors examine the following set of questions:

1. Is there not a need to conceptualize the relationship between form and content in order to discover forms of writing that can more adequately express our ideas?
2. Is the manifesto the form of public address most appropriate to post-critical philosophy of education? Or is there another form that is present yet occluded here behind the manifesto… something I am calling the declaration?
3. If so, what are the features of the declaration and how can these formal features come to shape your principles anew?
4. And is there perhaps something inherently educational about declarations? If creeds come from religion, charters from the law, and manifestos from politics, ethics, and aesthetics, then perhaps the authors have hit upon a form that is itself inherently educational, and thus needs to be cared for just as much as the content of the writing….

These questions are not meant to merely critique or affirm the project, but rather to love that which is most precious about it: the potentiality of the form. And it is my argument that this potentiality has yet to be fulfilled and must be cared for. Indeed, it must be protected, for like all emerging forms, it is also at risk of being lost before it is even recognized.

2

A Sociologist's Conversation with the "Manifesto for a Post-Critical Pedagogy"

Olga Ververi

A novel idea or point of view or perspective always seems prima facie quite appealing and fascinating. Depending on the field or area of interest it is associated with, it fills us with hopes and aspirations for improvement and effectiveness, for a better present and future — to put it plainly. "Faith in progress"[1] is the motto of modernity; however, it seems to remain deeply rooted even in today's culture. The "Manifesto for a Post-Critical Pedagogy" aims at exactly this: suggesting a new educational paradigm that promises improvement and progress in educational thought, research, and practice. The manifesto has been conceived by philosophers of education, however, it is addressed to researchers and academics of all disciplines of education, including sociologists. The following discussion stems from a sociological perspective and aims at examining the manifesto mainly politically and ideologically, but also theoretically and practically.

If an educational paradigm is a crystallized framework of theories, model problems, and solutions — to borrow Kuhn's

---

1   Luc Ferry, *La plus belle histoire de la philosophie* (Paris: Robert Laffont, 2016).

terminology[2] — or foci and analytical methods, then it seems that "Post-critical Pedagogy" aspires to become one. That is to say, it seeks to become a different way of approaching, researching, and interpreting education.

The four principles comprising the pillars of the new paradigm imply four inadequacies of the dominant educational paradigm(s) and their underlying philosophies: lack of principles; hermeneutical pedagogy; critical pedagogy; and cruel optimism. These are viewed by the authors of the manifesto as the ills of educational thought today. In addition to this, several theorists and philosophers are cited in the manifesto, offering in this manner the theoretical underpinnings of post-critical pedagogy as well as the analytical suggestions and orientations for research. The manifesto is rather effective in communicating briefly the main principles of post-critical pedagogy and its rationale. However, we should ask whether post-critical pedagogy is sufficiently convincing as a new paradigm that will change the way we currently think about education, and whether it has a practical value for the sociology of education.

As a sociologist of education myself, I am deeply interested in the politics of representation and meaning. The word *politics* should not be taken literally in this context nor should it be linked with any kind of power, or any illicit interests lying behind the manifesto. The authors of the manifesto are exceptional colleagues and dear friends and their motivation is purely scholarly. However, in academia we all try to find our niche in research and, as already stated, we remain quite obsessed with the modernist ideals of originality, novelty, and progress. So, in this sense, the manifesto operates in three distinct ideological manners. First, it is addressed to the academic community and aims at gaining support and legitimacy. Second, it challenges existing educational paradigms, which are thought to be dominant by imposing certain meanings regarding the purposes of education, the orientation of research, and the interpretation

---

2   Thomas S. Kuhn, *The Structure of Scientific Revolutions* (Chicago: University of Chicago Press, 1976).

of educational processes. And third, it is an "action-oriented" discourse[3] despite the authors' claim that they are not dictating "that we ought to do x" when they mention their position regarding principles.

Focusing upon the second and third points, I would like to examine in more detail the counter-meanings they ascribe to education and the action they propose:

1. In their critique of the poststructuralist and postmodernist accounts of the politics of identity, they suggest "*speaking and acting together*" in place of not speaking on behalf of anyone.
2. In their critique of critical pedagogy, they suggest *hope* in place of a utopian future emancipation, the latter viewed as an act of patronization with sentiments of superiority and hate.

The first meaning seems to be about methodology, and although "speaking together" might refer to how each one makes sense of their reality according to (social) constructivism, it is not clear what "acting together" means. In this sense, methodologically, post-critical pedagogy does not seem to suggest something new and, moreover, the suggestion for action is rather vague.

The second meaning of *hope* stands in opposition to the "emancipatory paradigm" and critical pedagogy in particular. What is interesting is that the authors of the manifesto seem to repeat some familiar allegations. More specifically, the authors claim:

> It enacts a kind of hermeneutical pedagogy: the educator assumes the other to lack the means to understand that they are chained by their way of seeing the world. The educator positions herself as external to such a condition, but must **criticize the present and set the unenlightened free** (cf. Plato's cave).

---

3   Terry Eagleton, *Ideology: An Introduction* (London/New York: Verso, 2007).

In reality this comes down to reaffirming one's **own superior position, and thus to reinstalling a regime of inequality.** There is no real break with the status quo.

Moreover, the external point of view from which the critical pedagogue speaks is through and through chained to the status quo, but in a merely negative way: the critic is driven by the passion of hate. In doing so, she or he surreptitiously sticks to what shall always be. Judgemental and dialectical approaches testify to this negative attitude.[4]

What I think is rather striking in the extract above is that the emboldened passages can be found in thousands of texts — not necessarily relevant to education — criticizing the political left. Should the left or critical social theory or critical pedagogy be immune to critique? The answer is *no*; however, the repetition of such standard allegations over the very "nature" of critical social theory and its movements (e.g., political left, labour/civil movements, educational paradigm of critical pedagogy) is totally pointless. It is like accusing liberalism of its basic principle of individualism. One can either accept or reject individualism. However, what one cannot do, is convince liberals of the ontological primacy of social collectivity. In a similar manner, for critical pedagogues, *power,*[5] *hegemony,*[6] *social stratification and exploitation,*[7] as well as the ideal of social justice are core

---

4   Emphasis added.

5   See, inter alia, Steven Lukes, *Power: a Radical View* (London/New York: Macmillan, 1974); Norbert Elias, *What Is Sociology?* (New York: Columbia University Press, 1984); Michel Foucault, "The Subject and Power," *Critical Inquiry* 8, no. 4 (1982): 777–95; Barry Hindess, "Power, Interests and the Outcomes of Struggles," *Sociology* 16, no. 4 (1982): 498–511; Pierre Bourdieu and Jean-Claude Passeron, *Reproduction in Education, Culture and Society,* trans. Richard Nice (London: Sage, 1977).

6   See, inter alia, Antonio Gramsci, *Selections from the Prison Notebooks of Antonio Gramsci,* ed. Quintin Hoare (New York: International Publishers, 1999); Stuart Hall, "Gramsci and Us," *Marxism Today* (June 1987): 16–21.

7   See, inter alia, Karl Marx, *Capital,* Vol. 1 (Harmondsworth: Penguin, 1976); Max Weber, *Economy and Society,* 2 Vols. (New York: Bedminster Press, 1978).

concepts driving their research interests and analytical methods. For this reason, they will always choose to "criticize the present" rather than identifying the positive aspects of education as shaped by liberal philosophies and ideologies. The latter approach, which is about identifying positive aspects of education, could be associated with the educational paradigm of *functionalism,* positing that education has a positive role in maintaining stability in society. Hence, in this sense, post-critical pedagogy could be viewed as providing a coinage for functionalism and the rhetoric of consensus.

Moving to the second allegation, that of the "superiority" critical pedagogues are assumed to have, this should again be examined in terms of critical social theory. *Ideology* and *naturalization of social reality*[8] are two concepts with which critical pedagogues are obsessed. So, I personally do not tend to view critical pedagogues as having a patronizing position towards e.g., students, parents, teachers, policy makers, and governments. I tend to regard them as having a theoretical specialization and expertise, which, in their view, allows them to analyze educational phenomena and reveal social relations of oppression and exploitation that are not "visible to the naked eye." I tend to think of them as I think of e.g., a cardiologist specialized in heart diseases, or a plumber who knows how to fix my tap. To give an example, I never thought of my plumber as patronizing me when he explained to me that faulty pipes resulted in low water pressure in my house. Why should I feel patronized if a critical pedagogue "revealed" to me why, for example, assessments are not "natural" components of the educational process?

Moving to the third allegation, according to which critical pedagogues' critique is viewed as driven by the "passion of hate." Again, this might be addressed in terms of the philosophical and theoretical underpinnings of critical pedagogy (see e.g., Marx's notion of *class hatred*). Hence, it seems to me that what the authors of the manifesto disagree with is *critical social theory*

---

8   See, e.g., Roland Barthes, *Mythologies* (Paris: Editions du Seuil, 1957).

itself, which indeed does not have at its core the concept of love, but the ideal of social justice.

To sum up, post-critical pedagogy seems to be methodologically akin to constructivism, philosophically affiliated to functionalism, and theoretically unsympathetic to critical social theory. Its core concepts of *hope, optimism,* and *love* seem to give a spiritual orientation to this educational paradigm rather than a political one. In this sense, I think that the adjective "post-critical" is indeed quite accurate and to the point, and seems to encompass the idea of reconciliation of humanity with the parallel suspension of any conflict.

To return to my initial question, whether post-critical pedagogy is sufficiently convincing as a progressive and applicable educational paradigm, I would say that from the perspective of the sociology of education the answer is binary. Post-critical pedagogy could be an interesting option for those in favour of the consensus view of society, ignoring economic, social, and cultural differences and conflicts of interests. However, for those of us who choose to focus on social problems (e.g., the impact of austerity in society, the impact of cuts in education funding and social welfare, the effect of adult unemployment in children's education, refugee children from Syria lacking education), I would say that post-critical pedagogy is not well-timed. In addition to this, what is missing from the manifesto is a more representative outline of the social and political context within which post-critical pedagogy is situated. In particular, the claim that "it is time to acknowledge and to affirm that there is good in the world that is worth preserving" is a rather partial view of contemporary reality and as such post-critical pedagogy seems to be a rather elitist educational paradigm.

However, what I find rather useful and important in post-critical pedagogy is the defence of "education for education's sake." Unfortunately, one of the main foci of sociology of education is *social mobility,* perceived as an indicator of equality of opportunity. This kind of research seems to legitimize the dominant educational model, which prepares children for the world of employment against the liberal idea of education known as *paideia*. Social mobility is *ab initio* a rather reactionary notion because it fetishizes the so-called middle class, presupposes the perpetuation of disadvantaged classes (e.g., working class), justifies individualism, and, finally, does not challenge the status quo nor social stratification. So, even for many sociologists, the purpose of education is reduced to a means for personal economic success. However, this instrumental view of education stands in absolute opposition to the Freirean purpose of education as leading to "conscientization" and "praxis." Consequently, I believe that post-critical pedagogy has much to offer sociologists of education and could enable them to redefine education, not in terms of what education is, but what education *should be*.

3

Towards a Pedagogical Hermeneutics
A Response to the "Manifesto for a Post-Critical Pedagogy"

Norm Friesen

The manifesto authored by Hodgson, Vlieghe, and Zamojski outlines five principles for a "Post-Critical Pedagogy." The first principle is that there are indeed principles to defend, and the second, that a *pedagogical hermeneutics,* rather than what might be called a critical "hermeneutics of suspicion,"[1] is now needed in education. Correlatively, the third principle calls for the end of critical pedagogy, and the fourth and fifth principles for a broadly affirmative "hope in the present" and "love for the world." Rather than seeing pedagogy's principle task as a critical negation and transformation of the world, Hodgson, Vlieghe, and Zamojski call for the affirmation of elements in the present as worthy of being passed on to future generations.

In his initial response to this manifesto, Tyson Lewis objects to the programmatic criticality of the manifesto specifically as a genre or form. Taking the *Communist Manifesto* of 1848 as his key example, Lewis sees this form or genre as entailing a deliberate critique that is diametrically opposed to the post-critical aims

---

1   See Rita Felski, "Critique and the Hermeneutics of Suspicion," *M/C: A Journal of Media and Culture* 15, no. 1 (2012), http://journal.media-culture.org.au/index.php/mcjournal/article/viewArticle/431.

of Hodgson, Vlieghe, and Zamojski. However, I believe that such an argument ignores the possibilities realized, for example, in the absurdist ironies of the 1918 *Dadaist Manifesto* or the self-aware post-humanism of Donna Haraway's 1984 *Cyborg Manifesto*.[2]

Understanding the "Manifesto for a Post-Critical Pedagogy" as following in the path of these later documents, I wish to elaborate on what I see as its two pivotal affirmations: an affirmation of a "pedagogical hermeneutics," and of a passionate hope in and for the world. I discuss the ontological, existential roots of these principles, referencing the existentialist hermeneutics of Heidegger and Gadamer, and an account of pedagogical hermeneutics from Helmut Danner. I begin, however, with a 1983 "modern classic" in pedagogy, *Forgotten Connections: On Culture and Upbringing* (translated in 2014 by the author of this response) written by Klaus Mollenhauer, whose ideas, I believe, are closely linked if not indispensable to the manifesto.

Mollenhauer emphasizes a return to the basic constituents, to the "elementaria" of modern education, and introduces his text by framing "the first question for education" as follows: "Why do we want children" at all?[3] Stated more broadly, Mollenhauer is probing why we as adults want children, and why we as educators want to work with children and young people. One answer to this question is that children give us hope for a different and better tomorrow — and the reference to hope in this answer resonates with the affirmation of hope in Hodgson, Vlieghe, and Zamojski's Manifesto. However, Mollenhauer emphasizes a rather different response — namely that I have or am with children and the young because "I want to perpetuate the (perhaps very little) goodness in my life."[4] This is an answer,

---

2 Tristan Tzara, "Dadaist Manifesto" (1918), http://391.org/manifestos/1918-dada-manifesto-tristan-tzara.html#.WRJkteXytaQ; Donna Haraway, "A Cyborg Manifesto: Science, Technology, and Socialist-Feminism in the Late Twentieth Century," in *Simians, Cyborgs, and Women: The Reinvention of Nature* (Routledge: New York, 1991).

3 Klaus Mollenhauer, *Forgotten Connections: On Culture and Upbringing*, trans. Norm Friesen (New York: Routledge, 2014), 8.

4 Ibid.

Mollenhauer continues, that not only implies an affirmation of the continuance of human history and human endeavors but also confirms the belief that "the way of life I offer to children has some common value."[5]

In speaking here of a "way of life [*Lebensform*]," Mollenhauer does not mean one's personal, ethical values and commitments, as much as he does a way or form of life, *sensu* Wittgenstein, who famously asserted that "to imagine a language means to imagine a form of life."[6] In these terms — in terms of the implicit patterns and values we embody, articulate, and act out every day — engaging in education in the broadest sense is all but unavoidable. As parents and educators, even simply as adults in public life, we embody and exemplify a way of life to children and young people, we perform a tacit affirmation of certain values, arrangements, and relationships. "Even the most radical" critic of education and society, Mollenhauer argues, "cannot avoid embodying an adult way of life in front of children; like any adult, he or she powerfully exemplifies one way of life or another for a child."[7] We cannot not be involved in a way of life much as we "cannot not communicate."[8]

Indeed, in various ways, children and young people force us to direct our actions toward them, and to make our responses intentional and deliberate, and in this sense also pedagogical. For example, we may be especially watchful when a young child appears to be wandering into traffic, or to the top of a staircase; we may feel compelled to help a homeless teenager or to guide a struggling sophomore or graduate student away from unnecessary problems and pitfalls.

How we decide to act in such contexts is where the question of pedagogical hermeneutics comes in. This is not hermeneutics

---

5   Ibid.
6   Ludwig Wittgenstein, *Philosophical Investigations*, rev. 4th edn., trans. G.E.M. Anscombe, P.M.S. Hacker, and Joachim Schulte (Hoboken: Wiley-Blackwell, 2009), § 19.
7   Ibid.
8   See Michael Winkler, *Klaus Mollenhauer: Ein pädagogisches Porträt* (Munich: Beltz, 2002), 12.

in the sense of a science of textual or Biblical interpretation, but refers to explication or interpretation (*Auslegung*) as "the basic form of all knowing,"[9] as the "procedure that we in fact exercise whenever we understand *anything*,"[10] to quote from both Heidegger and Gadamer. Interpretation in this sense is a concrete way of being in the world, a fundamental part of how we engage in the world purposefully and with concern. Heidegger observes that we are beings who are "constituted as care."[11] We work interpretively and self-interpretively according to our purposes and concerns — whether we are reading a paper, watching another's actions on the street, or wondering about a friend's recent words. Except that in the case of pedagogy — unlike reading a paper or pondering a recent remark — our care, concern, or purpose is of a particular kind. It is not motivated by pleasure, curiosity, or self-interest but, as Helmut Danner emphasizes, by *responsibility*.[12]

This implies a wide range of things. First, it implies that relationships that are pedagogical in nature — unlike friendships and other peer affiliations — are marked by an asymmetry between the one who takes responsibility and the other for whom he or she is responsible. At the same time, however, this does not mean that the one who is responsible is not also vulnerable, fallible, and in a position to learn from the one for whom he or she is responsible. Second, the temporality of the concerns and intentions associated with this responsibility are also bifurcated in a particular way: they are oriented simultaneously to the child's present well-being and to his or her future — a future conceived through hope as the realization of the potentialities

---

9   Martin Heidegger, *History of the Concept of Time: Prolegomena,* trans. Theodore Kisiel (Bloomington: Indiana University Press, 2009), 260, emphasis added.

10 Hans-Georg Gadamer, *Truth and Method,* trans. Joel Weinsheimer and Donald G. Marshall (New York: Continuum, 2013), 280.

11 Martin Heidegger, *Being and Time,* trans. John Macquarrie and Edward Robinson (New York: Harper & Row, 1962), 362.

12 Helmut Danner, *Methoden geisteswissenschaftlicher Pädagogik: Einführung in Hermeneutik, Phänomenologie und Dialektik* (Munich & Basel: Ernst Reinhardt Verlag, 2006), 98–123.

(and also the limitations) that may be apparent in the present. Third, it implies that pedagogy is concerned with the world or subjectivity of the child — even if this simply involves recognizing a child's or teenager's likely innocence of the dangers of traffic or of life on the street. This has been referred to as the child's *Eigenwelt,* his or her "own" world, just as a mathematical *Eigenwert* refers to a given entity's intrinsic value. The "*Eigenwelt* constitutes the horizon of understanding of the child,"[13] which like one's own interpretive horizon undergoes change over time, and hopefully expands through increased awareness of one's own fore-understandings and prejudice.

Of course, this is only the briefest sketch of how a pedagogical hermeneutic — a hermeneutic whose "creation" is called for in the Manifesto — might initially be articulated. Further interpretation and reflection would have the task of exploring, questioning, and reformulating some of the structures or regularities outlined above, and of continuing to uncover further fore-understandings or prejudices. In teaching practice, Danner maintains that a pedagogical hermeneutics would entail the cultivation of "openness"[14] — an openness that, according to Gadamer, "always includes our situating the other meaning in relation to the whole of our own meanings or ourselves in relation to it."[15] Significantly, in this context, students would no longer be configured as "learners" whose natural epistemic processes are to be causally or probabilistically explained, facilitated, or accelerated; nor would they be seen as an instantiation of "the other," brought into proximity through an absolute passivity and a transcendent respect.

Pedagogical hermeneutics as discussed by Hodgson, Vlieghe, and Zamojski is indeed not an ethical or epistemological "problem to solve." Instead, it represents the opening up of a space for reflection on and deliberate involvement in the dynamics of the intergenerational reproduction and reconfiguration of

---

13   Ibid., 114.

14   Danner, *Methoden,* 111.

15   Gadamer, *Truth and Method,* 271.

values, meanings, and of material and other aspects of culture. And given that children — to say nothing of our own social natures — demand such participation, open awareness, and reflection, a pedagogical hermeneutics of this kind is a matter of no small degree of concrete exigency.

4

Differences That Might Matter?
A Manifesto Diffractively Read

Geert Thyssen

To write a manifesto is to expose oneself—to make oneself vulnerable to critique. In the case of a co-authored piece, it is also to show oneself to one's co-writers (colleagues and perhaps friends). Yet, such vulnerability, which is moreover a vulnerability to one's self, forces one to take a close look in the mirror, and this includes those who are invited to deliver a reply as well. I find myself in that fortunate position. It is indeed with much gratitude to, and respect for, Naomi, Joris, and Piotr (and with equal humility) that I offer the following thoughts on their "Manifesto for a Post-Critical Pedagogy." Hastily assembled as they were "then," and clumsily put on paper as they are "now" to reflect the spirit of the actual reply, they are theirs and the reader's to further critique.

On to my first thoughts, then, which I believe were to ask the question of why we needed yet another manifesto, while hinting at the inevitable political dimension of a manifesto. There are some notable historical examples of clearly political manifestos, such as the 1776 *United States Declaration of Independence,* which served as an inspiration both for the 1789 *French Revolutionary Declaration of the Rights of Man and Citizen* and the 1790 *Manifesto of the Province of Flanders*—a little nod to fellow-Fleming Joris—but also the 1848 *Communist Manifesto* and the 1919 *Fascist Manifesto*. No less political, in the (post-?) feminist domain, seemed to me Donna Haraway's 1984 *Cyborg Manifesto*,[1] which I have become intrigued by while working on collaborative research on body–machine entanglements in the field of education.[2] In this domain, it is hard not to reference the "Manifesto for Education" issued by Gert Biesta and Carl Anders Säfström in 2011.[3] That manifesto aimed "to speak out of a concern for what makes education educational," and to address "the question of how much education is still possible in our educational institutions."[4] Perhaps, like the manifesto considered here, it was both ambitious and modest in scope, and understood, if anything, as "an ironic form — or as an ironic performance — [...] an attempt to speak and, through this, create an opening, a moment of interruption."[5] In any case, a few things struck me while (re-)reading the "Manifesto for a Post-Critical Pedagogy" *diffractively through* that of Biesta and Säfström. Perhaps these terms warrant a brief explanation.

Rather recently, and thanks to Joyce Goodman,[6] I have become intrigued by the work of Karen Barad, and particularly by the diffractive approach she develops in *Meeting the Universe Halfway*.[7] This approach builds on the writings of quantum physicist Nils Bohr concerning "diffraction." As a "physical phenomenon," the latter figures both in classical physics and in

---

1 Donna Haraway, "A Cyborg Manifesto: Science, Technology and Socialist-Feminism in the Late Twentieth Century," in *The Cybercultures Reader,* eds. D. Bell & B.M. Kennedy (London/New York: Routledge, 2000).

2 Frederik Herman, Karin Priem, and Geert Thyssen, "Body_Machine? Encounters of the Human and the Mechanical in Education, Industry and Science," *History of Education* 46, no. 1 (2017): 108–27.

3 Gert Biesta and Carl Anders Säfström, "A Manifesto for Education," *Policy Futures in Education* 9, no. 5 (2011): 540–47.

4 Ibid., 540.

5 Ibid., 542.

6 See, for example: Joyce Goodman, "Circulating Objects and (Vernacular) Cosmopolitan Subjectivities," *Bildungsgeschichte: International Journal for the Historiography of Education* 7, no. 1 (2017): 115–26.

7 Karen Barad, *Meeting the Universe Halfway: Quantum Physics and the Entanglement of Matter and Meaning* (Durham/London: Duke University Press, 2007).

quantum physics.[8] Classical physics sees it as "to do with the way waves combine when they overlap and the apparent bending and spreading of waves that occurs when waves encounter an obstruction [...], including water waves, sound waves, and light waves."[9] It does not consider it as pertaining to particles "since they cannot occupy the same place at the same time."[10] Quantum physics, however, has pointed to diffraction patterns in the form of "wave behaviour" in particles and to "particle behaviour" in waves.[11] Crucially, "diffraction patterns" point to "the indefinite nature of boundaries,"[12] and as theories of quantum mechanics apply not only to electrons and atoms, that is, to matter of the smallest size, but also, in fact, to all matter of the cosmos, Barad argues that there may be something to be gained from using diffraction as a prism through which to engage with all "naturalcultural practices."[13] Used previously by Donna Haraway as a metaphor to denote a way to figure "critical difference within,"[14] Barad sees a diffractive approach in research as "a way of attending to entanglements in reading important insights and approaches through one another in ways that help illuminate differences as they emerge: how different differences get made, what gets excluded, and how those exclusions matter."[15]

It is against this background that I have attempted to read Naomi, Joris, and Piotr's manifesto through that of Biesta and Säfström in search of that which Barad calls *differences that matter*.[16] I would like to present some differences I have noted as question marks, as *differences that might matter*. One such difference relates to specific recurring vocabulary. Whereas in

8   Barad, *Meeting the Universe Halfway,* 71–72.

9   Ibid., 74.

10 Ibid., 81.

11 Ibid., 83.

12 Ibid., 135.

13 Ibid., 32, 49, 90, 135.

14 Donna Haraway, "The Promises of Monsters: A Regenerative Politics for Inappropriate/d Others," in *Cultural Studies,* eds. L. Grossberg, C. Nelson, and P. Treichler (London/New York: Routledge, 1992).

15 Barad, *Meeting the Universe Halfway,* 30.

16 Ibid., 36.

Biesta and Säfström's text the word "freedom" predominates, in the "Manifesto for a Post-Critical Pedagogy" one reads about "hope," "belief" (that is, belief in the possibility of transformation), "love" (love for the world), and "care" (care and protection). Obviously, these words have quite particular meanings, historically and philosophically. To me it seems there is a distinctly religious feel to this set of words[17] — and this aligns with the choice of five principles — five being one of those numbers that has particular religious significance in the Western world (hence, for example, the "five senses" one supposedly has.)[18] Like Biesta and Säfström's freedom, I guess hope, belief, love, and care are conceived of *relationally* here: anchored in a sense of "commonality." Still, I wonder whether a notable difference in word choice here points to an enduring tension enshrined within the post-Enlightenment education project, namely, that between secularization and sacralization — a tension that is perhaps better not thought of in such binary terms, let alone framed within a presentist, teleological lens. Having previously touched upon this tension in my research, and thereby hinted at the religious in the secular,[19] I would be curious to know to what extent the post-critical pedagogy proposed is in fact religiously inspired. I assume it is no longer conceived of as a salvation project, but then what is it conceived of precisely, and might there be some religious dimension to that conception?

Another difference between Biesta and Säfström's manifesto and the one considered here that intrigued me as an historian of education is to do with time. In Naomi, Joris, and Piotr's manifesto we read about hope for "what is still to come," about

---

17 See, in relation to hope, e.g., Oliver Bennett, "The Manufacture of Hope: Religion, Eschatology and the Culture of Optimism," *International Journal of Cultural Policy* 17, no. 2 (2011): 115–30.

18 Geert Thyssen and Ian Grosvenor, "Learning to Make Sense: Interdisciplinary Perspectives on Sensory Education and Embodied Enculturation," *The Senses and Society* 14, no. 2, Special Issue (forthcoming, 2019).

19 Geert Thyssen, "The Stranger Within: Luxembourg's Early School System as a European Prototype of Nationally Legitimized International Blends (ca. 1794–1844)," *Paedagogica Historica* 49, no. 5 (2013): 625–44.

the/a "status quo" (i.e., "neo-liberalism"), and about "good in the world worth preserving," whereas Biesta and Säfström in their manifesto hint at the tension between the "what is" and "what is not" of the "here and now," in which one needs to stay within an "atemporal" approach that nevertheless takes "education as fundamentally historical — that is, open to events, to the new and the unforeseen — rather than as an endless repetition of what already is or as a march towards a predetermined future that may never arrive."[20] In that the manifesto analyzed here affirms "the value of what we do in the present" and stresses the need to create a "space of thought that enables practice to happen anew," it arguably shares with that of Biesta and Säfström an "interest in an 'excess' that announces something new and unforeseen."[21] But in also being concerned with the potential of the present for the future, unlike Biesta and Säfström, Naomi, Joris, and Piotr seem to linger not in the tension between "what is" and "what is not," but in that between "what alas is no longer" and "what is hoped to come." Indeed, the very name of the post-critical pedagogy project seems to embody and perform a *harking forward* to a *future past*. The present is defined either in terms of its (future) potential or of its (out-dated) inertia (the current/given "order of things"), and the closer one comes to the final parts of the manifesto, the more its stress on the "possibility of transformation" appears to be counteracted by a stress on things "worth preserving." To me it seems that both making the present pregnant with hope and reducing it to the status quo entails an emptying of the present as a "gathering" of possibilities in which order and disorder imply each other.[22] I would also argue, however, that working with(in) the tension of "what is" and "what is not" in education, as Biesta and Säfström advocate,[23] does not and need not remove temporality from the very conception of education. Again, Barad's diffractive approach might point to a

---

20 Biesta and Säfström, "Manifesto for Education," 541.
21 Ibid.
22 Tim Ingold, *Lines* (London/New York: Routledge, 2007). The idea of "gathering" he uses derives from Heidegger.
23 Biesta and Säfström, "Manifesto for Education," 541.

different conception of time/temporality in relation to education: one that emerges in "processual historicity" as "an open process of mattering through which mattering itself acquires meaning and form through the realization of different agential possibilities."[24] In such a conception of time as a manifold of "entangled" (mutually constitutive) agencies ("intra-actions"), a diffractive approach to education crucially shifts attention to "effects of difference" resulting from "knowledge-making" and other "practices we enact [that] matter — in both senses of the word" (both materially and discursively).[25]

This brings me to a final difference spotted and perhaps worth pointing to, which is to do with the attention paid in Naomi, Joris, and Piotr's manifesto to "subject matter": the study of, or initiation into, purely "for its intrinsic, educational, rather than instrumental, value" is associated with education proper. True to what Piotr mentioned during the seminar at which the manifesto was presented, the "pedagogy" it proposes is "poor in a Masscheleinian sense,"[26] in that it "does not specify tools or outcomes," not even in relation to that subject matter, but rather focuses on "the experience of education." In their turn, Biesta and Säfström refer to "a number of ways of speaking and doing and thinking about education that [...] run the risk of keeping out or eradicating the very thing that might matter educationally,"[27] but even more so perhaps than is the case here, their text is concerned with form — "forms of theory and theorizing" whose "resources are ethical, political, and aesthetical in character"[28] — rather than with content. Again, with Barad's work and her "posthumanist performative account of the material-discursive practices of mattering" in mind,[29] I am left wondering whether it is at all possible to reflect on educational

---

24 Barad, *Meeting the Universe Halfway*, 141.

25 Ibid., 71, 72, 91.

26 Cf. Jan Masschelein, "E-ducating the gaze: the idea of a poor pedagogy," *Ethics and Education* 5, no. 1 (2010): 43–53.

27 Biesta and Säfström, "Manifesto for Education," 543.

28 Ibid., 542.

29 Barad, *Meeting the Universe Halfway*, 146.

experience without "incorporating" into that reflection "tools" co-constitutive of that "experience," that is: all *matter*, not just subject matter, that matters and perhaps *should matter in education*. Indeed, to conclude my response to Naomi's, Joris's, and Piotr's manifesto, I would like to pose a provocative question: where and how do the "materialities,"[30] or (other) bodies shown to have been anything but marginal to projects of education across time and space,[31] figure within a post-critical pedagogy? What statute and functions does such pedagogy attribute to educational technologies? Or to the hands and feet, the eyes, ears, noses, and skin of those involved in education? In Barad's view, such (material-discursive) "bodies" (and co-constitutive agencies) "intra-act" as part of "dynamic (re)configurings of the world."[32] When "asking again what education, upbringing, school, studying, thinking, and practicing are," then, perhaps it is also worth reflecting on material-corporeal dimensions to these processes in a "posthumanist" vein. Inspiration for this could well be found in Donna Haraway's *Cyborg Manifesto*, the first chapter of which she considered "an effort to build an ironic political myth faithful to feminism, socialism, and materialism."[33] Politics, irony, and faith: *a perfect marriage à trois?*

---

30   Martin Lawn and Ian Grosvenor, *Materialities of Schooling: Design–Technology–Objects–Routines* (Oxford: Symposium Books, 2005).
31   Catherine Burke, ed., "The Body of the Schoolchild in the History of Education," *History of Education* 36, no. 2, Special Issue (2007).
32   Barad, *Meeting the Universe Halfway*, 169.
33   Haraway, "A Cyborg Manifesto," 291.

5

The Post-Critical Mind as a Gateway to Embodied Hope and Love for the World

Oren Ergas

Philosophy, like science, can be seen as an overarching term that refers to diverse ways of posing and engaging with questions. The development of these ways of questioning can lead to growing expertise and depth, but it can also create a growing fragmentation, expressed in siloed "schools of thought" that fail to engage with each other. When the latter movement becomes too strong, there is a risk that the ethos of philosophy, and most of all philosophy of education, will be betrayed, as a "school of thought" might miss the bigger picture when it becomes engrossed in its own game. I read Hodgson, Vlieghe, and Zamojski's manifesto as a diagnosis of this problem within the discourse of critical pedagogy and critical theory. This diagnosis and their call for action have far-reaching implications for educational theory and practice writ large. In this response, I will elaborate this claim briefly, and then offer a very brief sketch of my own attempt to heed the call of this manifesto.

Hodgson, Vlieghe, and Zamojski call on us to consider the relationship between critical theory and education. Broadly, they argue that critical theory's over-emphasis on critique may have been eclipsing *hope,* as the very condition that makes education a reasonable act. As they rightly argue, hair-splitting accounts of our world's maladies and struggles alone, illuminating as they might be, do not seem to offer such hope. Education certainly requires a response to relevant issues of inequality and oppression raised by critical theorists; nevertheless, there is also a need to introduce a balancing positivity into the *ways* in which critique itself responds to them. This manifesto is thus a call to resituate critique in relation to education, by asking us to examine the role and the actual *value* of critique within education. "Post-criticality," in the sense I read here, is not the renouncing of critique, nor a naïve flight to Utopianism, nor the advocacy of specific *ways* in which to engage in critique. Rather, it is a reminder that critique, in as far as it relates to education, should have a normative orientation — the enhancement of hope and love of the world. Such a proposal requires a shift in the premises from which critique stems as well as in the *educative* place to which it is to lead. It is a shift from criticality in which struggle yields more struggle, to post-criticality in which we acknowledge struggle but stress its dialectical entanglement with hope and love for the world. I view this post-critical turn, at least within philosophy of education, as a call to make pragmatic use of critique within education, which repositions education in its ethical roots. This is not critique for the sake of critique, but rather critique whose value is measured by how much it offers hope rather than despair, and love for the world rather than mere struggle.

The challenge for this kind of *post*-criticality is in avoiding two pitfalls to which Hodgson, Vlieghe, and Zamojski point: over-negativity that leads to despair, and unsubstantiated romantic Utopianism. There is a challenge here also in the justification for the word "post," which I interpret as a call to offer ways of critique that move beyond those deployed currently within critical discourse. The only way I know for doing so is overcoming the siloed "schools of thought," "Tower of Babylon" effect; that is, to recruit ideas and practices from other "schools of thought" in order to challenge the premises on which critical discourse stands. It is to this challenge that I will dedicate the remainder of this response as I heed the call of this manifesto by offering paths of affirmative action.

Hodgson, Vlieghe, and Zamojski suggest that critical discourse has not been critical enough of the educative (or perhaps un-educative) effects of its negative sentiment. I would point to an additional uncritical blindness within critical discourse — a blindness to the source of critical discourse's critique itself — the critic's own mind. In depicting inequality, violence, and oppression, critical discourse has been invested in identifying such issues within the world, namely (and arguably), "the known." Largely, critical discourse tends toward the opposite of so-called "navel-gazing." It engages in "social-gazing." My critical question is: what about the know*er*? What about the mind that engages in critique — the one that is writing now, and the one that is reading *this* word? A fruitful path for educational post-criticality, I argue, can be developed by introducing balance into the critique of the "known," by incorporating the critique of the knower.

No object, concrete or abstract, is known directly. What we call experience is experience as represented by particular embodied minds — you, I, her, him. Minds are fundamentally shaped by the social context into which they happen to be born, hence the seeds of social reproduction exist in society just as much as they exist in the mind. As I suggest, the libertarian ethos that lays in the roots of critical theory can be fulfilled not only by working with violence, inequality, oppression, "out there" in the world, but also by working directly with embodied minds that represent them "in here." Thus, the critical perspective I offer here proposes that the mind itself can be a site of embodied oppression, inequality, and negativity. Hope and love for the world can be found within a practical mode of critique that challenges the mind that sees, and not only what it sees. This perspective is grounded in schools of thought and practice, such as Buddhism, Taoism, Greco-Roman philosophy, and phenomenology, which can be applied toward social critique. These schools of thought can serve the manifesto's call, by proposing post-criticality through a contemplative mode of critique, which can also rejuvenate critical discourse by bringing in novel perspectives that break down its siloed nature. Very briefly, there are two modes of engaging in such *post*-critical pedagogy.

The first challenges our minds' ways of seeing, and points to the contingency of social construction. It entails a first-person methodical introspection referred to as mindfulness practice, which is broadly present in diverse contemplative practices. While mindfulness has recently been receiving much attention within educational discourse, as a way to reduce stress and enhance students' concentration, it is also known as a practice by which an individual can practice detachment from his or her own views and thoughts. Practicing mindfulness in this sense is not thinking, nor a form of thinking about thinking, which are characteristic of a critical stance. Rather, mindfulness is a mode of attention that acknowledges thoughts as real phenomena, yet not necessarily as true. Much of our thinking life is governed by content that concerns our social identity as it reflects issues of gender, race, equality, and so on, which all constitute the heart of critical pedagogy. Mindfulness is a practice in which one cultivates detachment from these thoughts, thus deflating their power. By reducing the grip of these social constructs over one's modes of being, knowing, and acting, mindfulness offers hope, for it can develop a more liberated agency that can then manifest in active engagement in social equality.

The second modality actively cultivates positive socio-emotional dispositions, such as hope, kindness, compassion, and love of the world, based on certain contemplative practices. This modality builds on the faculty of imagination. Post-criticality is reflected here in the acknowledgement of the mind as a locus in which negativity and despair in the face of the human condition appear constantly. However, this very mind itself can deliberately intervene when negativity becomes unproductive as a mode of critique. Here, one actively cultivates a positive attitude that acknowledges, indeed as Hodgson, Vlieghe, and Zamojski suggest, that there is good to be preserved in this world. In this case, the good to be preserved begins with certain dispositions of the mind that sees the world, which can then manifest in a motivation to engage in positive social change.

The above is merely a sketch. It is hardly a how-to guide that enables us to get out there and actively engage in this educative post-criticality. I, as well as many others, have been elaborating these ideas in far more detail in other publications.[1] More than anything, this is a response that argues that Hodgson, Vlieghe, and Zamojski's manifesto lends itself to novel theoretical and practical perspectives that remain rooted in a critical sentiment in a way that affirms hope and love for the world as fundamental grounds of education. With their offering of post-criticality, these scholars not only push the envelope of critical discourse and reposition it in an educative ethos, they also contribute to the overcoming of philosophy's "tower of Babylon" syndrome, as they make room for diverse schools of thought to contribute to this *post*-critical educative turn.

---

1   See, e.g., Oren Ergas, *Reconstructing "Education" through Mindful Attention: Positioning the Mind at the Center of Curriculum and Pedagogy* (London: Palgrave Macmillan, 2017).

6

Love for the World in Education

Stefan Ramaekers

In my response, I will not go into the manifesto as such, or as a whole. I will limit myself to responding to the authors' claim that "[w]hen we truly love the world, our world, we must be willing to pass it on to the new generation," which is a reference to (a short transcription of) Hannah Arendt's (by now, I guess) famous passage where she brings together education and love for the world: "Education is the point at which we decide whether we love the world enough to assume responsibility for it and by the same token save it from that ruin which, except for renewal, except for the coming of the new and young, would be inevitable."[1]

Having referenced this passage before myself,[2] I must confess I never seem to have bothered to actually try to articulate what Arendt meant by "loving the world enough." I guess the larger, overall argument she is developing in that text, "The Crisis in Education," forms some kind of encompassing background in which this passage is embedded, such that one no longer feels necessitated to explain this any further, as if this passage logically follows from what she says before. But the stronger tone of

---

1   Hannah Arendt, "The Crisis in Education," in *Between Past and Future: Eight Exercises in Political Thought* (New York: Penguin Group, 2006), 193.
2   See Stefan Ramaekers and Judith Suissa, *The Claims of Parenting: Reasons, Responsibility, and Society* (Dordrecht: Springer, 2012), 138.

assertion with which Hodgson, Vlieghe, and Zamojski use the expression "love for the world," which is inherent to the kind of text they have written, does seem to necessitate such explanation. Or at least, it invites a series of reflections and questions that can, rather simply, be summarized by the following two questions: "What (kind) of love?" and "What world?"

I am not sure what to make of the connection Hodgson et al. are making in saying "When we…, we *must*…" (emphasis added). Their account of love for the world entails that we, as educators, *should* relinquish our hold on the world. What kind of claim are they making in relation to the love for the world they are arguing for? Put differently, what is the nature of the commitment ("must") they attribute to this love? I read the sentence I singled out as suggesting, or implying, that it "naturally" follows from our love for the world that we pass it on to the next generation and leave it in their hands. But is that necessarily so? Is it somehow internal to love, naturally given in love, that when we love something we are then also willing to give it out of our hands? Phenomenologically, love comes (and goes) in many guises, and has many registers (of depths and shallows), as we all know.[3]

Love can be possessive (as in erotic love, for instance); it can be characterized by a longing to devour the object of one's love, and so one may not be willing to share this object with others.

Love can be "mixed with resentment and intimidation,"[4] and if it is such a mixture then the object of our love may not be something we love wholeheartedly, or with full devotion, for it

---

3   A more obvious way of responding perhaps might have been to go into the discussion of education and (Platonic) *eros,* probing into the inherent (or not) educational character of (what the authors call) love for the world, and asking the authors to be more explicit about this and relate their account to (some account of) *eros*. I chose not to. Instead, I found it more interesting to raise a few issues in relation to some of the many shapes love can take phenomenologically.

4   The example is taken from Stanley Cavell. He is using it in the context of his account of what it is a child learns when learning language. I cannot (and do not need to) go into Cavell's account of teaching and learning a language here. I'm only borrowing his example. See Stanley Cavell, *The Claim of*

may also, simultaneously, be something we are indignant about; it may also, simultaneously, be something we feel threatened by.

Love can be romantic. And when it is, it is blind, as the well-known saying goes. Here, I am reminded of what Nietzsche says about love when writing about Christianity in *The Anti-Christ*: "Love is the state in which people are most prone to see things the way they are *not*. The force of illusion reaches a high point here, and so do the forces that sweeten and *transfigure*. People in love will tolerate more than they usually do, they will put up with everything."[5] Most commonly, I take it, this is understood in negative terms, suggesting that lovers are in denial of reality, not "seeing" what outsiders, such as their friends, can "see" about the other person. Lovers typically do not see one another's shortcomings. (A measure of friendship may well be the friend's capability of delicately balancing the line between speech and silence on this matter. But that aside.)

Love can also be praiseworthy. There may be, that is, a register of the commendable or praiseworthy characteristic of love, as Nietzsche also seems to suggest in the passage just quoted. Lovers "put up" with many things, "tolerate more" than in relation to someone else, simply because they love the other. The blindness of love here, then, is not something that happens to the lover and brings her in to a state of denial, but may be something that bears the characteristics of an act of will. The lover's blindness may be something she willingly submits to.[6] Cavell seems to touch upon this when, in his discussion of skepticism, he says the following:

> To live in the face of doubt, eyes happily shut, would be to fall in love with the world. For if there is a correct blindness, only

---

Reason: Wittgenstein, Skepticism, Morality, and Tragedy (New York: Oxford University Press, 1979), 177.

5   Aaron Ridley and Judith Norman, eds., *Nietzsche. The Anti-Christ, Ecce Homo, Twilight of the Idols, and Other Writings,* trans. Judith Norman (Cambridge: Cambridge University Press, 2005), 20.

6   I take it something of this is captured in the saying "turning a blind eye to something."

love has it. And if you find that you have fallen in love with the world, then you would be ill-advised to offer an argument of its worth by praising its Design. Because you are bound to fall out of love with your argument, and you may thereupon forget that the world is wonder enough, as it stands. Or not.[7]

The blindness of love may very well be something worthy of (in need of?) cherishing. There is a price, Cavell seems to say, for wanting to see, or wanting to see too much, or more generally, for wanting to argue (explain, give reasons) for one's love for the world. The danger is that we no longer find ourselves enchanted by it, perhaps cannot even imagine any more what it was like to be enchanted by it. Looking at something in wonder, either silently or not, doesn't seem to bear an inquisitive stance. The objectification the latter implies may make one intolerant. "Or not."

Love can be many more things, I guess. I want to ask, therefore: In education, what kind of love are Hodgson et al. talking about? What is it, in love, that "makes us" want to pass the world on to the new generation? Or that naturally invites (or seems to naturally invite) a willingness to pass it on? And what is it, in love, that makes us want to pass the world on to the new generation without qualification?

This brings me to my second question: "What world?" The authors are quite upfront when they say that "[i]t is time to acknowledge and to affirm that there is good in the world that is worth preserving." I also would like to believe there is good in the world that is worth preserving. But this is clearly begging the question. It doesn't seem philosophically very sound to just say that "[i]t is time to etc…" without further qualification as to what that is. Is Star Wars something they would consider as something an educator can love (in whatever sense they take this)? Is it something they consider to be part of "the world" — the world we as educators are willing to affirm and pass on to the new generation? And what about *South Park*? Or football? Or reading? Or *Macbeth*? Or Rambo? Or friendship?

---

7   Cavell, *The Claim of Reason,* 431.

Or friendship as conceived by Facebook? Or mobile phones? Or Brexit? Or Trump's election? Or maternity leave? Or... And, in any of these cases, if yes, then why? If no, then why not? What criteria are invoked then?

Maybe I'm being unfair here. Maybe I shouldn't be asking for very concrete, specific things when the authors are speaking about "the world." Maybe I should be talking about it in a more general sense. So, consider the following example. Recently, Gwendolyn Rutten, the chairperson of the Flemish Liberal Party (Open VLD), when promoting her new book *Nieuwe Vrijheid* (*New Freedom*), fiercely defended "our way of life" — "our" meaning: "Western European." She even called this way of life "superior." Of concern to her are the fundamental values buttressing the liberal constitutional state: freedom, equal rights, separation of church and state, etc.[8] Needless to say, this stirred up quite some reactions, from people criticizing her claim to superiority of "our" way of living (and the grounds of this claim), to people pointing out the many things going wrong in our Western way of life (suicide rates, medication abuse, burn-out, etc.). But I think it can be safely said that she truly loves the world she's living in, and that she finds that we must (be willing to) pass it on to the next generation, and not allow, for example, the world espoused by radical Islam to displace "our world." She clearly thinks something is under threat and is in need of preservation (to refer to words used by Hodgson et al. in their manifesto).

I'm wondering, therefore: is this an instance of the "good in the world" that Hodgson, Vlieghe, and Zamojski would like to acknowledge and affirm? Are they loving the same world as Rutten?

---

8   Cf. "Onze manier van leven is superieur aan alle andere," *De Standaard,* April 22, 2017, http://www.standaard.be/cnt/dmf20170422_02846090.

POST-CRITIQUE

Post-Critique
A Conversation between Naomi Hodgson, Joris Vlieghe, and Piotr Zamojski

Having read the excellent and thought-provoking responses to our manifesto, we gave a lot of thought to how to respond to and do justice to them. We definitely didn't want to write separate replies for each of them, and we really wanted to keep the conversation going between us, the authors of the manifesto, and those who wrote such generous and carefully crafted responses to our text. So, we decided that the three of us would each make some written notes on the replies, which we then shared and took as a starting point for a face-to-face conversation. What follows is a text that is largely based on the transcript of that conversation, but that also draws from our own preliminary notes. The conversational form naturally entails some repetitions and returns to earlier threads, as well as rough shifts in the flow of the argument, and these are reflected in what follows. Hence, it is not as smooth as a standard academic text. As it was a conversation in which we were discussing the responses of our colleagues, we refer to them, and to each other, by given (first) names.

Piotr Zamojski: I thought that we could start our conversation by talking about the exercise of reading the responses to our manifesto and preparing our answers. How did you find this exercise? I ask you this because I found this a very interesting exercise in itself. For me, the two most important questions addressed to us in the responses are those posed by Stefan: *What is the world? And what is love?* Indeed, "the world" and "love" are key concepts for the standpoint we aimed to express. What do you think about these questions, and about Stefan's response?

Joris Vlieghe: I don't think it's helpful to start from referring to love in an interpersonal sense. When Arendt talks about love for the world, she obviously means something different.[1] For instance, when Stefan problematizes our notion of (passionate) love for the world/subject matter, he uses examples of love for particular persons, which are indeed partial, blind, prone to jealousy, etc. I don't think this is a convincing argument. Educational love has to do with caring for things, and this is, precisely, highly impersonal. For that matter, educational love should also not be mistaken for the passionate zeal of the political activist.

Another point that Stefan makes, with Cavell, is that of the irrational aspect that comes with each form of love (and also with love for the world, we should admit). If I understand him correctly, the point at which we are no longer willing to critically interrogate what we care about is the moment when we fall together with the things in question, and Cavell metaphorically names this moment "falling in love." That is, something comes to a halt. However, in our understanding of love, irrational as it is, love is a *beginning* (in so far as it interrupts a given order of things). Above all, it is a call for continuous work and responsibility (which we take, different from what Tyson says in his response, to be a deeply educational concept): one has no choice but to make it [the world] into an object of attention, interest, and care for the new generation. This is, at the same time, a vulnerable gesture, as it means that the new generation can begin again with it in an infinite number of ways. More positively, to educate out of love is a matter of giving and setting free

---

1   Hannah Arendt, "The Crisis in Education," in *Between Past and Future: Eight Exercises in Political Thought* (New York: Penguin Group, 2006).

our common world. In that sense, there is a connection between education and politics. Political action is, probably, impossible without educational transformation. But, it doesn't make sense to reduce, for this reason, education to politics (i.e., claiming that education should be for political change). But on that note, I think Naomi and myself might have different interpretations of the Cavell quote that Stefan is referring to. When I read your notes, Naomi, it seems you have a more positive understanding of what Cavell has to say about love.

Naomi Hodgson: I am not sure "positive" is the right word, but yes, I found that there was some sort of similarity between our use of it [the idea of love] in the manifesto, and what was going on there [in the Cavell quote], because of the idea of blindness.

PZ: But this is a "correct blindness."

JV: So blindness can be good — to put it very bluntly?

NH: Yes. Love for the world does not in any sense imply a denial that anything bad is going on in the world or with the world, it doesn't require that you choose to ignore this wrong. But, for Arendt, it was about "loving the world enough"; it's not falling in love with it, and being unable to criticize it. Arendt's statement, cited by Stefan, seems to encapsulate that education is precisely premised on hope: "Education is the point at which we decide whether we love the world enough to assume responsibility for it and by the same token save it from that ruin which, except for renewal, except for the coming of the new and young, would be inevitable."[2] What form of responsibility is entailed in moving on from "the point at which we decide whether we love the world enough" with a will to educate? If we decide that we do love the world enough — that there is something of it that we feel is of value to pass on or protect — this entails the willingness to pass it on. If we are willing to pass it on, responsibly,

---

2 Ibid., 193.

73

this implies that we do love it enough (in spite of its faults). But what is "it" that we love? To take a phenomenological approach to answering what we mean by love and the world does not necessarily lead us anywhere. To suggest an equation with erotic love, of a possessive kind, points to a love for the world that is conservative, fundamentalist, essentialist, perhaps (cf. the book by Rutten that Stefan refers to. She wants to pass on the world as it is, i.e., as she sees it ought to be). Hopefully it is clear that this is not what we have in mind.

It is perhaps the blindness usually associated with romantic love, expressed positively by Cavell (cited by Stefan), that comes closer to capturing the relationship between love, education, and the world in Arendt, and in the manifesto: "To live in the face of doubt, eyes happily shut, would be to fall in love with the world. For if there is a correct blindness, only love has it. And if you find that you have fallen in love with the world, then you would be ill–advised to offer an argument of its worth by praising its Design. Because you are bound to fall out of love with your argument, and you may thereupon forget that the world is wonder enough, as it stands. Or not."[3] What this draws our attention to, I think, is that love is not the only emotion according to which we view the world: but education requires that we *love the world enough* to be willing to pass it on.

JV: So what you are suggesting here is taking the same quote that Stefan has used in a different direction?

NH: Yes, I think that quote does not necessarily contradict what we are trying to do. But I think Stefan does raise an important point about this use of Arendt's idea of love for the world. Because it really has become something of a trope in recent writings in educational philosophy. Many people refer to that specific bit of Arendt, without necessarily unpacking what it means. So I found it helpful — at least for me — to try to pick up that

---

3   Stanley Cavell, *The Claim of Reason: Wittgenstein, Skepticism, Morality, and Tragedy* (New York: Oxford University Press, 1979), 431.

criticism and ask what we actually mean, in the context of the manifesto, by "love for the world." And the Cavell quote was quite helpful in trying to articulate that. It is about loving the world enough to be able to go on with those mundane practices.

JV: So, what I said earlier might not have been entirely correct, or at least it might testify to the way in which I initially responded to the replies. With this I mean that I responded in a rather defensive way. I have tried to point out where our readers and commenters have read things wrongly or that they have read their own ideas in to our manifesto, so it is like I have tried to dot the i's and cross the t's. That was my feeling, but at the same time I thought it was worthwhile, because it gave me the opportunity to be more explicit about particular points.

PZ: Further to that, while reading the replies, I really got the impression that a manifesto is too short as a form in itself to get to grips with the ideas. And so, particular names, notions, and phrases can be interpreted in so many different ways that sometimes you could be really surprised by a reading of particular concepts, like the notions "hermeneutical pedagogy" and "pedagogical hermeneutics," which was rendered by Norm Friesen in his reply not entirely in line with our intentions.

NH: I was glad that the respondents each picked up different aspects of the manifesto. And I think you're right that the manifesto form is necessarily short and makes bold claims and statements that you don't have the space, or give the space, to fully justify. And so, in a few of the replies, the authors start off being very supportive of the claims we make in the manifesto, and then go off on a tangent that reverts back to the original critical position. Hence, I was concerned that my response was also quite defensive, and that I was writing in a way that kind of went against the idea of the manifesto. In the sense of saying, "You haven't really understood what we have written, let me explain that to you," and I wanted to avoid doing that. But at the same time, you want to have that opportunity to elaborate what it means to say "love for the world" or "separation of the educational and the political," precisely because you can't do that to the necessary extent in the manifesto.

PZ: Before we go deeper into this matter, let me just repeat and specify that for me reading the replies and commenting on them was a very interesting exercise, one that went against the dominant academic practices in these "publish or perish" times, that is, in times when one should write more than one can read and think. Most of the time, when we publish something, we get no response at all, it's like publishing into a void. What we write is usually lost in this universe of proliferating papers. So the way we have proceeded was exceptional: we had the experience of reading the replies and hence we saw that our colleagues really took the time to think about what we have written and to give a response. That was so enjoyable, and in a way it was also for me an existential experience of how wrong the academic world is these days.

JV: But now you are critical, not post–critical!

PZ: Yes indeed, in a way you are absolutely right, but on the other hand in doing this exercise, together with six other colleagues, we have retrieved what is really academic: commenting on each other's work.

NH: I agree. I made a note on that, after reading Tyson's response, which led me to think about what it is that we have actually made manifest. I would name this as a movement in thought in educational philosophy that is better articulated collectively, as a conversation, than as isolated publications towards individual research profiles, developed in contexts that increasingly lead us to question why we do what we do, the value of what we do, and the fact that it is assessed by criteria that do not belong to us or the matters at stake, i.e., not educational criteria. So how we've done it is also a part of what we make manifest.

PZ: I couldn't agree more! In that regard, I had an interesting experience while reading Oren's response which, contrary to its intentions, has awakened my "Hegelian" soul, so to speak, and reminded me of the origin of the idea to write the manifesto in the first place: more and more we have the impression that there is a shift in educational theory of which we are not yet aware.

JV: You even suggested that there might be a new *Zeitgeist* or, more correctly, *Weltgeist,* which I thought was a surprising but perhaps very accurate thing to say. Hence, I found it very interesting to play with the idea that our manifesto should not aim at changing people's minds, but that it is, first and foremost, the expression of the feeling that there are new ideas hovering in the air, so to speak.

PZ: Indeed, Oren's reply proves that there is something in the air, as you say. From various positions, using many diverse concepts, theoretical traditions, and ideas, theorists from all around the world are making visible efforts to express a new way, a particular way, of understanding education. Indeed, the first part of Oren's response aptly synthesizes the manifesto, but the second part relates to a tradition of thought that is completely unfamiliar to me, and so I found it difficult to understand. But, if people from theoretical backgrounds as different as Oren's and mine can — let me use Hegel again — recognize themselves in the manifesto, it means that it serves its purpose, and that maybe a shift in the "Spirit" is ahead of us. On that note, were there other interesting, significant, intriguing, or maybe even disturbing things in the replies we haven't discussed so far?

JV: Well, what I found fascinating — as you already hinted at — is that Norm rendered some of our ideas in a way that is not exactly what we meant.

PZ: Yes, I agree with that. I think there are two major misunderstandings between the position we sketch in our manifesto and the reading of it offered by him.

The first one concerns the difference between a political logic and an educational logic, and the question of mediation. Norm observes that: "Rather than seeing pedagogy's principle task as a critical negation and transformation of the world, Hodgson, Vlieghe, and Zamojski call for the affirmation of elements in the present as worthy of being passed on to future generations."

And then — at the end of his reply — he argues that educational responsibility is "oriented simultaneously to the child's present well-being and to his or her future — a future conceived through hope as the realization of the potentialities (and also the limitations) that may be apparent in the present."

I would say that this is not the case. In our manifesto — which is strongly influenced by Arendt's formulation of what is at stake in education — the *future* is a matter of risk. It is essentially unknown, and it is left to the new generation, and their inventiveness. Therefore, the future is not a realization of a potential that is visible now. Potential that has to flourish in the future, develop, grow stronger and greater, etc. Rather, it refers to an opening of pure potentiality[4] and hence it regards something unforeseen, incalculable, unpredictable. In that sense, education is always about a transformation of the world, but not about a particular transformation, and not about direct transformation. This is how we understand the Arendtian concept of renewing the world. The hope, though, lies in the present — not in the future: it is *a purely educational hope* that relates to establishing a thing in common between the generations, and the possibility of a rejuvenation of the world. Education, by making a subject matter into a thing of common interest, gives hope, here and now, that the world will neither wither from lack of interest nor be destroyed by people who would act without being introduced to it and knowing how it has worked so far. Or, as Arendt puts it: "But the world, too, needs protection to keep it from being overrun and destroyed by the onslaught of the new that bursts

---

4   Cf. Tyson Lewis, *On Study: Giorgio Agamben and Educational Potentiality* (New York: Routledge, 2013).

upon it with each new generation."[5] This entails that education is not interested in the child's *Eigenwelt* directly, as Norm suggests: this might be of interest in sociology or psychology. Education, as we understand it, is all about relating to the child's *Eigenwelt* through the mediation of a common thing, i.e., a subject matter, a part of the world that is being studied, thought about, and exercised with.

The second misunderstanding in Norm's reply concerns the difference between hermeneutical pedagogy — which, I think, Norm advocates for — and pedagogical hermeneutics. The latter is not an application of 20th-century philosophical hermeneutics to education, and it is not operational when a pedagogue has to invent her response to a child's being, as Norm puts it. Rather — as we have put it in the manifesto — by pedagogical hermeneutics we understand the core task of post–critical educational theory: rather than creating applicable means, or debunking existing educational reality, we want to draw attention anew to what we are doing as educators, what the essence of these doings is, what their immanent value is, but also that they increasingly become dwarfed, functionalized, instrumentalized, and deprived of their meaning.

JV: So, in that sense, the *Weltgeist* is maybe a split *Weltgeist*. With this I mean, a *Weltgeist* that is both still critical and at the same time post-critical *in statu nascendi*.

NH: Yes, I don't know if this is felt more specifically in educational philosophy than it is across the board in educational studies. Because one of the things that came out strongly, and especially in Olga's piece, was that the hold of critical theory and the hold of politics on educational theory is so strong. It seems fundamental to how critical research goes on. Perhaps our own orientation is clearer if we take a less direct approach. That is, if we say that our issue is not with critical pedagogy per se but a) with how it is taken up today in educational research and b) with

---

5   Arendt, "The Crisis in Education," 186.

our current context and the need to look again at how best to find a way to go on with it. Not to accept it, not to deny inequality and suffering, but to take seriously what Latour means when he says that "critique has run out of steam."[6] The constitution of prejudice and structural inequality is different now than it was when such theories proposed radical contestation to the status quo — and achieved huge shifts. For Olga, the concern seems to be, in part, that we are dismissing the concerns of critical pedagogy and critical theory and, in doing so, are turning our backs on the political issues that motivate them. But this — and I'm afraid this is an issue with theory that has long existed — implies theory to be an immovable thing, unaffected by the conditions in which it exists, and changes in the constitution of the objects of its concern. Thus, when Olga writes that the post-critical approach is "methodologically akin to constructivism, philosophically affiliated to functionalism, and theoretically unsympathetic to critical social theory," the implication is that this lack of sympathy is politically irresponsible, and the principles we set out are then swiftly assimilated in to existing paradigms. As Olga herself laments, sociology of education itself is political in its concern with social mobility and not, for example, with consciensization and praxis, in the Freireian vein, and so there is a need to think otherwise than in instrumental terms. The way in which this is expressed in the manifesto is precisely to respond to this by affirming the *educational* dimension of our educational practices. We could, of course, show more of the ways in which education today is marketized, privatized, data- and output-driven, and we will no doubt continue to do so in a certain manner. But we know this. The question is how we respond in educational terms — or perhaps better, in the name of education, in the name of what we hold as worthy of passing on — so as to protect these aspects of education. In doing so, we challenge ourselves not to default to cynicism, or outright despondency, as we do have a responsibility to find a way to go on.

6   Bruno Latour, "Why Has Critique Run out of Steam? From Matters of Fact to Matters of Concern," *Critical Inquiry* 30, no. 2 (Winter 2004): 225–48.

The manifesto, then, does not endorse a functionalism, call for stability, and seek consensus, as Olga suggests. She states that, unlike figures ordinarily associated with critical sociologies of education, such as Foucault, we do not seek a criticism of the present. But, as indicated above, the purpose here is a reorienting of critique from one that reveals a hidden "truth" (and therefore maintains the place of such critique in the order of things), to one that articulates those aspects of our current conditions that are left out of view by both dominant discourses and practices, and by the negative critiques that show us how we are oppressed by these. It is precisely out of a concern with the present — not a utopian or even dystopian future state — that we articulate these principles. I have argued elsewhere that the use of Foucault in educational research has remained within a Marxist understanding of power,[7] and this tendency is visible in Olga's response also.

PZ: I think what we have to state is that we are not against critical approaches to education. Let the critical inquiries go on; we are just looking for other strategies. That is the reason why we refer to Latour in the manifesto: since radical critique seems not to bring about any significant change in the order of things, maybe we should try something else.

JV: What I find difficult about that perspective is that the implicit message we are giving to our colleagues and friends whenever they make a "critical" point is, "Ok, you go to your office, and go on doing all your interesting work, but by no means tell us about it. When we meet, let's talk about the weather and not about our academic research."

---

7   Naomi Hodgson and Paul Standish, "The Uses and Misuses of Poststructuralism in Educational Research," *International Journal of Research and Method in Education* 32, no. 3 (2009): 309–26; Naomi Hodgson, "Researching Power and the Power in Research," in *Power and Education: Contexts of Oppression and Enabling,* ed. Antonia Kupfer (Basingstoke: Palgrave Macmillan, 2015).

NH: Yes, the danger is that positions are again relativized and we remain in our "siloes," as Oren states.

PZ: Alright, I just wanted to stress that the post–critical perspective is never possible without critical research. You have to be aware of the wrongs, in order to know how to care for the good in the world, not repeating the sins that are already being recognized as sins. That's why our stance is post–critical, and not anti–critical.

JV: Can I play the devil's advocate and be very critical? What you seem to say is, "Ok, we shouldn't be naïve; the post–critical has to take into account things that are wrong in the world, and therefore the traditional critical paradigm is very important." However, this seems to be a very dialectical position again. In a sense, we are dependent upon the traditional critical paradigm, in order not to be naïve.

NH: Perhaps this is partly a problem of what we mean by "post" in post-critical. One sense is that it's "post" because the critical did its massively important work, but we are living in a different time and it doesn't have the same purchase that it had before. So, post-critical necessarily comes after critical. A second sense is that the problem is not critical theory per se, but the way it is taken up in educational research, and the fact that that hasn't changed as conditions have changed. And so it's not necessarily that we are dependent on the entire body of critical theory and the paradigm, but that there is something in those texts that have something to say in this context.

JV: So maybe the problem with the critical paradigm is that, for many, still today it seems to be the be all and end all. Let me come back to Olga's contribution as an illustration. She approaches education solely from a critical-sociological angle. Taking this perspective, one rightfully only has the choice between two options: either to take sides with, or to expose and to denounce, a system that is through and through oppressive.

And so, Olga's critique comes down to saying that we, in view of our concern with transformation and our firm hope that things can be different, should join the critical camp, and that, in the end, we betray our starting point: the manifesto just contributes to the status quo and, more precisely, this is because we adhere to (what is presumed to be) an elitist account of education. As such we are advocating, in her reading, a functionalist view that serves the powers that be.

I believe we should not bring in as a defence that we do sympathize, politically speaking, with the oppressed. That is, from an educational point of view, immaterial. What matters is that education can transform us and that this is intrinsically worthwhile (and this is not dependent upon the place education plays in the larger societal context). Political change and educational transformation are altogether different things, and confusing both comes down to making, what analytical philosophers call, following Gilbert Ryle,[8] a category mistake. Educational transformation is good in and of itself. Asking for an external justification that explains why it is good is *missing its point.*

This is, again, not denying that in our contemporary world the way education is organized often supports oppression, and that there are good reasons to analyze our social world, inclusive of educational institutions, in terms of hidden power structures. The problem with this approach, however, is that it automatically implies that we need to reform those institutions and make them into an instrument for creating a better world. An attempt, that probably is bound to fail and that demands a constant call for reform, which is what we see happening today. Another way to put this, with Chesterton,[9] is that the sociologist only asks what is wrong with the world, and thus forgets to ask what is good — and thus worth preserving — about it. We claim that once one starts to play the game of criticism, one never gets out

---

8   Gilbert Ryle, *The Concept of Mind* (Chicago: University of Chicago Press, 1949).

9   Gilbert Keith Chesterton, *What Is Wrong with the World?* (London: Cassell, 1910).

of this entrapment. One has no choice but to denounce evil, oppression, and injustice. However, this is first of all a political concern, not an educational one.

In view of this, it could be said that Olga's account is itself a functionalist one: education serves political emancipation to such an extent that the educational evaporates. Likewise, our drawing attention to the logic behind critical approaches is not trivial, as Olga maintains. It is exactly pointing out that the critical-sociological perspective misses out the educational in education. The same applies to her argument that we — again — join the right-wing critique of critical pedagogy that each and every individual has the ability to think for herself and hence that the interference in her life by an enlightened teacher is by definition patronizing. In our view, this testifies to a blindness to the educational as such. When we call for a move beyond the platonic scheme of the student enslaved by ignorance and in need of a "master explicator," as Rancière puts it,[10] we do this *for purely educational reasons.* We agree that we can learn a lot from the plumber in the example Olga discusses, but this is, of course, not an educational situation. What is unique about education is the assumption of a radical equality that is indeed lacking in most other societal contexts and situations. This equality is guaranteed because teacher and student devote themselves to a subject matter to such a degree that both are under the authority of this thing (which makes them relate to one another as equals). Put otherwise: educational and sociological equality belong to different spheres of life.

PZ: However, if we would like to express the relation between a critical and post-critical perspective — which I think is also at stake here — we should refer to a phrase I found in Naomi's notes and which I found particularly important: "that we must ensure to distinguish hope from denialist optimism."

---

10 Cf. Jacques Rancière, *The Ignorant Schoolmaster,* trans. Kristin Ross (Stanford: Stanford University Press, 1991).

NH: When I wrote this, I was responding to what Oren was doing in his reply with the idea of mindfulness. He does draw on a rich Eastern tradition, but what he says is in line with a positive psychology discourse. My experience of this is that we should just go on, saying "It's all fine! Just think positively, it will all be fine!" This is exactly what I mean by denialist optimism. Oren's reply, however, captures the very work upon oneself that is required when seeking an educational, rather than a political, response to our conditions: an intervention in our own thoughts when we revert to cynicism or negativity. But it quickly moves again from the educational to the political in Oren's assumption that by correcting a negative disposition with a positive one, we can engage in positive social change. There is a risk here that hope becomes imbued with a positive psychological zeal. While mindfulness practice, in the rich sense that Oren invokes, may be one way in which a love for the world and affirmation of the present is made manifest today, this is not necessarily the inflection that is implied in the manifesto: we must — as you have noted — ensure to distinguish hope from denialist optimism. Whereas for Olga we are denying social inequality and injustice by our move from critical to post–critical, the move to mindfulness as affirmation of the present might effect its own denial.

PZ: In other words, perhaps we are dealing here with a continuum between two extremes: on the one hand, the denialist optimism of positive psychology and similar standpoints, which suppress the existence of the wrongs in the world, and, on the other hand, a radical critical perspective, which doesn't allow us to see anything positive at all, anything in the world that would be worthy of affirmation. What we are trying to do is to escape both of these extremes.

NH: So I think that we need to be clearer about what we mean by hope. Because, it is obviously ordinarily associated with optimism, and with "everything will be fine" — but I don't think this is what we mean.

JV: This reminds me of a recent book by Terry Eagleton, *Hope without Optimism*.[11] I think we could say — referring to Heidegger's well-known difference — that hope is an *ontological* dimension and optimism an *ontic* manifestation of a more fundamental attitude towards the world. In other words, optimism takes hope in a very particular direction, which may be completely unjustified, and so optimism is very often very naïve. But, different directions are possible.

NH: Relating what we have said about hope in relation to the separation of politics and education we advocate, I was formulating my replies to the responses on the morning of 9th June 2017, and it was difficult not to relate the notion of hope with contemporary politics. The Conservative Party had, overnight, to the surprise of many, including themselves, not won the UK elections (They had not lost it either, though). This was attributed in part to the electorate — including (reportedly) an increased proportion of young people (18–25-year-olds) who often don't bother to vote — voting for hope: hope that another politics is possible, hope that the unlikely might just happen. So, people voting on the basis of principle, in the collective interest, not just "what's in it for me?" and how it will affect the economy. There is no necessity in the current order of things; change, or at least disruption, is possible. This is not to overstate the events of the UK general elections; life and politics will remain within a certain parameter of recognizability. But something has changed. The so-called "post-truth" politics based on assumption and personal belief rather than reason and collective responsibility does seem to be wearing thin already, even though we do not yet fully understand its depths.

Twice in recent weeks I have started the day by having to tell my children that there has been an attack in the UK. The first took place in Manchester, at the end of an Ariana Grande concert attended largely by teenagers and their families. The second,

---

11 Terry Eagleton, *Hope Without Optimism* (London: Yale University Press, 2015).

less than two weeks later, was in London. In this context, what can hope mean? As a parent, trying to reassure the younger generation that it will all be fine, that they are safe, when actually, you don't feel able to say that with any certainty. It is perhaps in the face of this question that we can make sense of the strict division between politics and education in the manifesto: to try to educate for this context, or for a future context that, to the older generation, might look bleak, and from which we seek to protect our children, we already take it from them. In an Arendtian sense, to do so would be already to decide on how they should take care of the future. But how does this work in the context of family life, as opposed to the specific confines of the classroom? In the classroom, it makes sense to say that "educational and sociological equality belong to different spheres of life," as you put it earlier, Joris. In the familial context, no such separation, or "suspension," as Jan Masschelein and Maarten Simons call it, is possible.[12] Partly because the teacher–student relationship, particularly one founded on the assumption of equality, is of an impersonal nature (to some degree) in a way that the parent–child relationship could never be. Put simply, what distinguishes these relationships is love, in the interpersonal sense, as we discussed above. Or the form this love takes. The suspension, the working out how to move in the gap between past and future that we find in Arendt's articulation of the crisis in education, is oriented not to a crisis in our educational institutions or systems, per se, but to a crisis in upbringing. It is precisely the intergenerational relationship that Arendt is concerned with. What we mean by love for the world, then, now seems an obvious question to ask. As you said earlier, Piotr, the questions that Stefan raised were among the most important.

So, by bringing into play the current context, I wanted to put to the test whether and how the manifesto principles could make sense if we were talking about upbringing or the parent-child relationship. But also, in relation to the responses, I wanted to

---

12 Jan Masschelein and Maarten Simons, *In Defence of the School: A Public Issue* (Leuven: E-ducation, Culture & Society Publishers, 2013).

take seriously this concern that you get in Olga's response, and that I think would be a quite standard response to what we've done, which is "but what does this look like in reality, when you've got all this stuff going on? How do you actually make this real, when we are dealing with these kinds of questions that necessarily impose themselves on education?" So that was part of the reason for drawing on the current socio-political context, but also I wanted to wait until after the election to start writing, because with a different result, the idea of hope might have taken a different direction.

PZ: I think what is interesting in what you have just said is that you have tried to reply to the responses in a particular, exceptional context, which — in a way — brought all these ideas into everyday life. As mentioned before, the manifesto calls for retrieving the educational. And one of the profound educational notions we want to make manifest is exactly upbringing (rather than for instance, parenting). The meaning of this notion became strongly visible and is also problematized by the context that you have mentioned at the beginning of your comments [the UK elections and the terrorist attacks].

JV: Yes, I would say that what Piotr and I wrote in preparation for this conversation is more on a theoretical level and that it offers theoretical clarifications of the standpoint we defend in the manifesto, whereas you started from a very precise and concrete educational question: upbringing against the background of the very evil things we are confronted with today, and what it means to educate in such a context. What unites our three perspectives, however, is a particular notion of *time* that informs our manifesto — to move on to another topic.

This has also been picked up by Geert and Tyson, in their responses. Hope in change is, they claim, predicated upon a denial of the present. I tend to disagree. This teleological perspective is exactly the time of political action: what Geert and Tyson describe is the tension between a present situation, which is the object of dislike and indignation, and a (never-to-come) future in which a better life is actualized. Education, on the other hand, produces a gap in such a teleological (and, hence, political) ordering of time. Love makes us forget about (this) time, and brings about a full concentration on the *here and now* — a full attention and devotion to the object of study, and nothing else.

PZ: Coming back to the relation between optimism and hope, I think that we simply cannot be very optimistic, especially in view of all the critical research that has been done in the field of education. But, on the other hand, we need to somehow struggle further, we need a purpose in education. In that regard, particularly in relation to Geert's, but also to Tyson's reply, hope shouldn't be conceived within an eschatological logic, i.e., as something that refers to a distant future that has to be accomplished (which means that the present is simply the time of waiting, dispensable time, time to be used — in the name of a "future-goal" to come). We are rather talking about *hope in the present*. When one is in an educational situation — e.g., studying something with one's students, or repeating some mundane doings with one's children — one has hope. These things make hope present; hope that the world will not perish and will be rejuvenated in some way.

JV: Yet another way to put this, more technically or philosophically, is that an eschatological take on hope deals with it as a "technical precondition for education." I refer here to an expression coined by a Dutch phenomenologist and educational philosopher, Martinus J. Langeveld (whose work has not been translated into English). For Langeveld, we can only educate because we rely on the fact that tomorrow things might be better. If we don't have that hope, our efforts are futile. But the criticism of this standpoint is that this is a merely instrumental account of hope. For me it has been very helpful to refer to the film *Le Fils* by the Dardenne brothers.[13] What the father/teacher does in

---

13 Jean-Pierre Dardenne and Luc Dardenne, dirs., *Le Fils* (Diaphana Films, 2002).

that film is embody hope in the present (instead of displaying a hopeful attitude in an instrumental sense). What the educator is doing in the present situation, as depicted in the Dardennes' film, is good and can make a change. It's not about planning ahead what might be happening tomorrow — there might be a disaster tomorrow, the boy might kill the father/teacher (or vice versa) — but that's not important. The important thing is that they do something together: they explore the world of wood-work, and that actually brings hope to the situation, because it changes something here and now.

PZ: If I could add something here referring to the issue of time that Joris mentioned just a minute ago. This is most important, especially in Geert's response, which refers to Biesta and Säf-ström's "Manifesto for Education," and asks about the relation between our manifesto and theirs.[14] Where we differ is precisely on the issue of time. It seems that the rejection of the time di-mension in education that Biesta and Säfström are proposing stems from the metaphysical understanding of time they have adopted. Indeed, conceiving time as a line linking past, present, and future, reduces education to a purely productive process that can be easily determined by the economy and subordinated to various political aims. However, this is not the only way one can understand time. And — I think — that a post–critical per-spective may be also rendered as regaining an educational sense of time. Referring to Agamben here, educational time is *kairos*, i.e., now–time, radically *present* time, which he opposes to the traditional *chronos*–conception of time that underlies Western metaphysics.[15] It is true, however, that we didn't emphasize this enough in the manifesto itself: education is an event of *kairos*, it suspends the work of normal, metaphysical, productive time (*chronos*), makes it inoperative, and makes all engaged in educa-

---

14 Gert J.J. Biesta and Carl Anders Säfström, "A Manifesto for Education," *Policy Futures in Education* 9, no. 5 (2011): 540–47.

15 Giorgio Agamben, *The Time that Remains: A Commentary on the Letter to the Romans* (Stanford: Stanford University Press, 2005).

tion experience a radically different flow of time, which arises in the profound absorption of attention by the subject matter. In that regard, I think that Biesta and Säfström are right in their diagnosis: if you think about time in metaphysical terms, as a "past–present–future continuum," and when you think about education using this concept of time, you are turning education into some kind of productive process, structured within a continuum of "intention-process-and-product."

What we are trying to do, in the manifesto and in developing a post–critical educational philosophy — as Joris and I recently did in an article on Agamben and Badiou[16] — is to appreciate the present as such. Naomi, in my view, did something similar in her article — written with Stefan — on Haneke's movie *Die Siebente Kontinent/The Seventh Continent*.[17] In a very controversial way, you have interpreted the movie by leaving its ending outside of consideration (an ending that can impose itself as the meaning of the film), and by solely focusing on the family and their doings as *presented* to the viewer throughout the film. More exactly, you didn't relate to the future of this family or, better, the lack thereof, in order to say something about the essence of family life as such. Family life, being a parent, being a child in a family, upbringing, all happen in the present. To put it differently: there are other ways to understand time, and what we simply try to do is to regain *educational* time.

JV: Likewise, we could take the example of the film *Le Fils* to a greater extreme. What the protagonist does in the Dardennes' film is, literally, give the future out of hand; in a sense, the father/teacher is not interested in what is going to happen in the future. As I said, things might go awfully wrong, but there is a moment when you are truly educating and you are not bothered

16 Joris Vlieghe and Piotr Zamojski, "The Event, the Messianic and the Affirmation of Life: A Post–Critical Perspective on Education with Agamben and Badiou," *Policy Futures in Education* 15, nos. 7–8 (2017): 849–60, DOI: 10.1177/1478210317706621.

17 Michael Haneke, dir., *Der Siebente Kontinent/The Seventh Continent* (Wega Film, 1989).

to be interested in the future. And, I think, from a phenomeno-logical point of view, it makes sense to say that when we teach, we lose control over time, i.e., over *chronos,* and hence that the future doesn't exist, or that it has no meaning at that moment.

NH: Or: the future doesn't explain the practices you are involved in at that time.

JV: Going back to the relation between Biesta and Säfström's and our manifesto for a moment, let me add that what — I think — is at stake in both texts is to retrieve the educational in education. Education regards the possibility of a fundamental change in our own and our collective lives in relation to a world (subject matter) we become attentive to. Education also regards relations between persons, a relationship towards the world, as well as techniques and practices that are particular and unique. These are not to be found elsewhere, and especially not in the sphere of politics. A political activist relates in a different way to the world than the educator does: whereas the first is driven by indignation and hate, the latter is infused with passion and love; whereas political techniques are all about mobilizing peo-ple against perceived societal problems, educational techniques aim at neutralizing the responsibility for solving these problems and at "slowing down,"[18] and making time and space, etc. What we essentially claim is that a critical perspective — even out of the best of intentions — tends to push the particularity and uniqueness of the educational under the carpet and to replace it by things that are not educational, properly speaking.

PZ: I think in view of the replies, but also referring to recent discussions we have had with the audience after presenting the manifesto on recent occasions, the idea of love for the world is predominantly understood in a very sentimental way and/or in relation to hate — as a rather dangerous political concept. So

18 Klaus Mollenhauer, *Forgotten Connections: On Culture and Upbringing,* trans. Norm Friesen (London: Routledge, 2013).

colleagues would typically respond to our manifesto: "nationalisms are expressions of love for a particular nation — is that what you want? Would that be a post-critical standpoint?" Of course not. Nationalist zeal is a form of love that is predicated on hatred towards other nations, and of "otherness" as such — and so it is not educational at all. In our view, education stems from a *purely affirmative relation to the world.* Now, the reactions we have received to our manifesto clearly show that love is indeed a complex and difficult notion that needs further clarification.

So let me come back to Stefan's response, which also testifies to this problem. I think that one can have doubts, as his reply shows, when one tries to understand love in phenomenological terms. To a certain extent this thread is present also in our manifesto, but essentially love in the post–critical perspective has an ontological meaning, signifying the labour of studying, thinking, exercizing. This is love for the world — not for a person. However, this love is twofold, as love for the world entails love for the new generation. It is so because only the new generation can rejuvenate the world. In that sense, a pedagogue loves her students — but if other ways of loving are engaged in that relation it is not *educational* love any more. Love for the world is testified by the teacher, who teaches her subject passionately and, in that sense, this particular way of loving is justified, it can be explained, and there are reasons that can be shared. This is why this love, common love, is not an individual feeling, but an attitude that can be shared with others. While exhibiting one's love, that is, while practicing the labour of study, thought, and exercise with a thing (subject matter), the teacher is not only providing reasons how and why this thing can be loved. She is also inviting her pupils to fall in love with it.

NH: But that's why — and I think both of you have remarked on this — the example of the politician (Rutten) that Stefan refers to in his response, doesn't actually work.

PZ: Absolutely, first of all this politician says that our tradition, i.e., Western civilization, is better. She uses the word "superior."

93

But "better" is not synonymous with "good" — the use of the former requires hierarchies. However, an educational logic doesn't entail hierarchies. It is based on the affirmation of the worth of a thing, a part of the world, which is simply worth studying. This is the thing we, the existing generation, would like to point the attention of the new generation to, just by saying, "Look, this is important, please take a closer look," instead of by saying "What we have is superior!." Moreover, passing on to the next generation doesn't mean indoctrination, but requires giving it away, letting it go. It implies a risky relation with the new generation: their attitude to the thing we offer them is not constrained by the need for conservation, but is opened to new, unforeseen uses they might invent. The world is to be rejuvenated, not replicated. I'm not sure this would be Rutten's intention. If our tradition is better, we shouldn't aim at rejuvenating it, we have to simply reiterate it, impose it on the new generation — which is a rather political than it is an educational point of view.

JV: I completely agree. In view of the transformative character of true education, Stefan's reference to Rutten's book is misguided, as what she advocates is exactly the opposite. She — being the leader of a political formation — wants to completely determine what the meaning of this common world is, for us and for the generations to come. Also, what seems to be at stake for her is — once more — a rather sociological approach vis-à-vis education: introducing the newcomers in what Arendt calls "the art of living," i.e., socialization. However, the idea of education articulated in our manifesto is much richer, and has first and foremost to do with the possibility that socialized norms, expectations, and identifications are temporarily suspended. However, let me make a small remark here, because — knowing the discourse of the political party she leads — I can imagine she would have immediately replied: "Yes, but it's only the Western tradition which allows for rejuvenation of the world. If we would live in Turkey or Iran, we would not be allowed to begin anew with the tradition." Maybe this is not an unimportant aspect, since an essential part of the Western tradition is that it also allows for going against the tradition.

PZ: I agree with the latter, but I have some serious doubts about the former.

JV: And so do I.

NH: And it would be a slightly cynical move [on Rutten's hypothetical part] to invoke critique as a defence of her conservative stance. I don't know who said this, but the opposite of love is not hate, it's "I don't care." It is indifference that is on the other side.

PZ; JV: Yes!

PZ: After having discussed the issue of love (and hate) to such a large extent, maybe this is the right moment in our conversation to come back to the other, but related question on which we briefly touched at the beginning: what exactly do we mean by "world"?

JV: There are many concerns to raise here. Obviously, one issue is as follows: if we claim that education should be based on love for the world, we always have to deal with the very practical question *what* we are going to teach, and to pass on. The other issue is that the word "world" implies some kind of totality: it refers to something of an enormous dimension, or something that encompasses everything. So how to define it? Of course, you could do it very superficially, i.e., in a geographical sense, which is of course not what we mean. Although, at the same time, in view of the problem of climate change, world might exactly refer to our planet. Furthermore: do we only include stuff that has been historically formed, of which the disciplines would be very nice illustrations: mathematics, history, carpentry, etc.? Or do we also include ways of life? In Norm's interpretation, on the basis of Mollenhauer, the world means exactly this: our way of life. And, as he goes on showing, we have no choice but to start from our own way of life, even if we deny this, and even if we don't want the new generation to follow our way of life. For him, and maybe also for Mollenhauer, the world refers first of all to the way in which we as a human community relate to the world and organize our living together on this planet. One way I've found fruitful in order to explain the concept of the world in Arendt is to refer to her Heideggerian background, that is, the idea that world always implies some kind of exteriority. According to Heidegger, we are thrown in to the world, we are born into something that is *already there,* and that is really objective, concrete. There is something out there, something that is beyond our own making, and yet we have to relate to it, although it's not fully under our control.

PZ: In that last sense, everything, including lifestyles and things, is a part of the world.

NH: Yes, but there is a distinction to be made there between that which is open to question (i.e., ways of life, cultures, and disciplines), and thrownness, which is not negotiable. We cannot escape it, it's there.

PZ: I find the question about this negotiable dimension of the world — i.e., what are the parts of the world that you are willing to pass on? — a political question, rather than an educational question. In other words, the question, what to include in the curriculum is for me a political question. Or, this is a question that regards the point where education and politics meet. In this respect, there is no final, universal, "firm" answer to the question "what is the world?" Posing this question to which we have no answer makes education a public matter, it raises the issue of education, which is constantly discussed and reflected on by society in the public sphere. In that regard, Masschelein writes that school is an invention that is "the time and space that society gives itself to reflect on itself when confronted with the new generation."[19] Again, we do not have an answer to that question, we are just pointing to the fact that what to include, what to teach is the central political question *about* education. We have no choice but to debate about this issue. Any selection regarding the things we invite the new generation to study, think, and exercise with is subject either to democratic debate, or to some kind of authoritative decision.

NH: I also think this relates to the question of the extent to which our manifesto is normative, and the extent to which that is a problem. Because for some people, in their responses, it is a problem — because there seems to be some sort of elitism implied, or there are some things that we want to protect, and other things that we wouldn't — and I don't think we have addressed that aspect of the manifesto as yet in our conversation. I certainly think we need to be clear on this point: that our manifesto is not normative in terms of the content, but it is normative in terms of an attitude, a way of proceeding — just at that very minimal level. But also, and I think this is an issue perhaps because respondents have tended to pick up on perhaps one principle, rather than taking the principles as relational. If you just take one, and take it to its full extent, then it doesn't necessarily reflect the entire attitude of the manifesto. For me, the principles are, rather, regulated by one another, but the responses are raising the question of whether this is a manifesto on what education is, or normatively, conceptually, what it should be.

PZ: I would say that it is neither.

NH: No, ok, but I think that how it is read: within this opposition.

PZ: For this reason I really think we must stress the following: the manifesto is addressing *what already is.* It is not normative in the sense that it is supposed to point out what these practices

---

19 Jan Masschelein, "Can Education Still Be Critical?," *Journal of Philosophy of Education* 34, no. 4 (2000): 603–16, at 613.

(e.g., education, upbringing, school, studying, thinking, lecturing, note-taking, and practicing) *should* be. They are already there. But they are not acknowledged, as they are being hidden from view by the dominant way of thinking about education, which reduces education to a matter of bureaucratic control and management in view of accountability and measurable outcomes. So what we have tried to do, is to say: "Look! These practices continue to exist, we are doing them, they are important, they constitute what education is all about, and so these are exactly what we should care about." Hence, the manifesto is neither normative — in the above mentioned sense — nor purely descriptive either.

NH: The responses are also asking, I think, whether the manifesto is methodological rather than practical? And what does it mean for educational-philosophical research?

PZ: In my view, this is exactly how I understand — and I hope you share this understanding — the role of theory in a post-critical perspective. What we have called pedagogical hermeneutics is neither practical nor methodological, but rather — paradoxically — it is both at the same time, since it refers to opening a way of speaking, thinking, and theorizing that allows people to act in a particular way, and to understand their own actions, to refer and relate to them, to defend them if needed, and to put into words why they are important. This desire for a pedagogical hermeneutics is, in my understanding, virtually present in the critical approaches towards education that abound today, such as the critique of the audit society, of the role of measurement in education, of the obsession with league tables, and so on: it is often argued that these — rightfully criticized — ways of grasping education *miss something* essential to education, but this "what is missed" is not so easily identified by these critical discourses. For me this is one of the main issues for post-critical pedagogy. This is how I read the attempts of Gert Biesta, Jan Masschelein, Maarten Simons, Tyson Lewis, and others; as actually articulating this unacknowledged essence of education. As attempts to make us again attentive to the thing that runs the risk of remaining absent in neoliberal arrangements of education. Following this, what we call for is not simply designing an effective method. I could recall here the idea of a "poor pedagogy" as suggested by Jan Masschelein. Post-critical pedagogy is poor in the sense that it doesn't offer any particular means regarding good teaching or conducting good educational research. However, it gives a meaningful horizon within which we can practice and understand what we are doing.

JV: Yes. By the way, you mentioned the term "poor" just now, which Tyson also uses as a possible alternative description of what we have done. What about the term "manifesto" for naming our project: are we intending to change it, following Tyson's suggestion, into a declaration?

NH: As far as I am concerned, I'm fine with the name "manifesto." I think we should acknowledge that, on the basis of what Tyson says, it should be called a "poor declaration," but I don't think we should change it.

JV: My main reason for sticking to the name "manifesto" is that the book project is about publishing what we did [at the launch] on 17th October 2016, and at that moment it was a "manifesto"...

NH: Quite. I think it still makes sense to call it a manifesto, since our project tries to capture something that exists and to put it on display, i.e., to make it manifest. It's not that we have made up a whole new theory, and that we try to get rid of the critical theory. There is rather a growing momentum to articulate a shift in the way we theorize education, as Piotr hinted at earlier on when talking about the contemporary *Weltgeist*.

PZ: Again, I think we have to emphasize that the intention behind the manifesto is really modest. We didn't try to say that we are going to introduce something completely different that will revolutionize the field.

NH: I think there is a certain sense that this was a bit of an arrogant move, to make these claims and write a "manifesto," but you are right, it wasn't our intention to claim that we have a brand new paradigm, as for instance Olga seems to suggest — a paradigm shift that will amaze everyone.

PZ: On that note, I think we can all agree with Tyson's comment that the form in which we choose to present our ideas matters a lot. The only thing I disagree with is the way he describes, or defines, what a manifesto is. I think Norm has also indicated that manifestos in the world of art are not, as Tyson seems to imply, necessarily referring to the future. Is the manifesto, as a form, essentially prophetic? Although I like very much the distinctions Tyson has developed in his reply (i.e., between creed, charter, manifesto, and declaration), I don't think that manifestos are what he claims them to be. The majority of aesthetic manifestos argue precisely what real art is — not what it should be in a better future. I would even say that perhaps the *Communist Manifesto* is an exception, even though it has dominated the public imaginary with its prophetic (eschatological) attitude. So, apart from Marx's and Engels's texts, isn't a manifesto mostly an attempt to manifest something, i.e., to make something that is present (in an *ontological* sense) present (in the *ontic* sense), as you put it earlier, Joris? And conversely, isn't a declaration — despite the beauty of the definition given by Tyson — always also the establishment of something: a country, an institution, a movement? Our intention is much more modest: we simply have come to a point where we felt that we had to make explicit a way of looking at education that we see emerging. In that sense, the manifesto is a retroactive attempt to articulate a view on education that already is there, and that we consider to be worth developing. It is tempting to agree with Tyson's rendering of declaration, but — I think — our intention was precisely to make manifest what is already there. Hence — manifesto.

JV: Although I am very sympathetic to the argument that particular forms have particular educational or non-educational consequences, I would also say that this very claim is a most anti-educational gesture. I say this because it comes down to arguing that a manifesto cannot ever be educational. And, this goes against what Tyson is saying himself, i.e., that we should profanate forms, and so give them a new use and new destination. Well, we tried to do that with the form of the "manifesto." Tyson seems to exclude this from the very start by saying: manifestos are one category, declarations are an altogether different category, and so on. In that regard, we should even be able to write a profanated creed. Moreover, what we try to do is change the attitude from one of a desire to force upon an evil world a certified bright future, to one that is all about starting to relate affirmatively and attentionally to the world as it stands. "Manifesto" exactly means what it originally refers to: the fundamental educational act of showing something, to make it present — here and now.

Contributors

Oren Ergas is a Senior Lecturer at Beit Berl College, Israel. His publications focus on contemplative practices in education, educational philosophy East/West, and the implications of neuroscience for teaching, learning, and the curriculum.

Norm Friesen is Professor in the Department Educational Technology at the College of Education, Boise State University, USA, where he teaches and advises in the doctoral program. Besides translating the modern pedagogical classic Klaus Mollenhauer's *Forgotten Connections: On Culture and Upbringing,* Friesen has written and edited books on e-learning and media in education and is currently collaborating on an Introduction to Human Science Pedagogy.

Naomi Hodgson is Lecturer in Education Studies at Liverpool Hope University, UK, where she teaches and researches in philosophy of education. Her research focuses on the relationship between education, governance, and subjectivity. Her publications include *Philosophy and Theory in Education: Writing in the Margin,* with Amanda Fulford (Routledge, 2016), *Citizenship for the Learning Society: Europe, Subjectivity, and Educational Research* (Wiley, 2016), and the forthcoming *Philosophical Presentations of Raising Children: The Grammar of Upbringing,* with Stefan Ramaekers (Palgrave, 2018).

Tyson E. Lewis is an Associate Professor of Art Education at the University of North Texas, USA. He is author of several books, including *On Study: Giorgio Agamben and Educational Potentiality* (Routledge, 2013).

Geert Thyssen is Senior Lecturer in Education and Early Childhood Studies at Liverpool John Moores University, UK. He is currently co-editing, with Ian Grosvenor, a special issue of the journal *The Senses and Society* entitled "Learning To Make Sense: Interdisciplinary Perspectives on Sensory Education and Embodied Enculturation."

Stefan Ramaekers is Associate Professor in the Laboratory for Education and Society, KU Leuven, Belgium. His publications include *The Claims of Parenting: Reasons, Responsibility, and Society*, with Judith Suissa (Springer, 2012) and the forthcoming *Philosophical Presentations of Raising Children: The Grammar of Upbringing*, with Naomi Hodgson (Palgrave, 2018).

Olga Ververi is Lecturer in Education Studies at Liverpool Hope University, UK. Her current research focuses on citizenship education teaching and learning through the prism of the concept of the "sociology of critical thinking."

Joris Vlieghe is Assistant Professor in educational theory and philosophy, KU Leuven, Belgium. His current research deals with the impact of digitization on the meaning of education and on the transformations this implies for school practices. He is also interested in developing a post-critical approach to teaching in terms of a passionate love for a subject matter.

Piotr Zamojski is a Lecturer in philosophy of education at Liverpool Hope University, UK, and adjunct lecturer in educational theory at the University of Gdańsk, Poland. His research interests include the relation between totalitarianism and educational theory, the Holocaust and education, the making of solidarity, post-critical pedagogy, and post-critical philosophy for education.